take the plunge 2

31 MORE DAYS
To Deepen Your Faith

LAWRENCE POWELL

Scripture taken from the New King James Version®. Copyright © 1982 by Thomas Nelson. Used by permission. All rights reserved.

Scripture quotations marked MSG are taken from THE MESSAGE, copyright © 1993, 2002, 2018 by Eugene H. Peterson. Used by permission of NavPress. All rights reserved. Represented by Tyndale House Publishers, Inc.

Scripture quotations taken from the Amplified® Bible (AMP),
Copyright © 2015 by The Lockman Foundation
Used by permission. www.Lockman.org

Copyright © 2019 by Lawrence Powell

All rights reserved. No part of this publication may be reproduced in any format or by any means without permission, in advance, from the author.

ISBN: 978-1942705918

Published By:
Lawrence Powell,
Agape Family Worship Center
P.O. Box 1623 - 501
East Hazelwood Avenue Rahway,
New Jersey 07065

Printed in the United States of America

Dedication
Take The Plunge 2

Thanks to God the Father for all He's done and continues to do in my life and ministry. I can only encourage others to Take the Plunge because of the countless times and ways the LORD has encouraged me to do the same—come what may, in good times and bad.

Thanks to each of you who surround and support me constantly. I love and appreciate you more than I can possibly say.

Likewise, many thanks to my family for standing with me and loving me unconditionally. I adore you!

Finally, thank you Adria, Aaron, Ashlyn—and Skylar. You are absolutely amazing!

Contents

Take The Plunge 2

Catch The Vision

Day 1 - Use Your Imagination 2
Day 2 - Greater Is He in You 8
Day 3 - The Voice of the Lord 12
Day 4 - Dreams Really Do Come True 17
Day 5 - Deceisions Determine Destiny 22
Day 6 - There's a Treasure in You 27
Day 7 - The Invitation Still Stands 32
Day 8 - You Have Potential 37
Day 9 - There Is a Way Out 42
Day 10 - This Is Your Day 47

Get Moving

Day 11 - If You'll Do This, Then I'll Do That 53
Day 12 - Five Things You Should Know on the Way Up 58
Day 13 - Don't Be Deceived 63
Day 14 - Keep It Real 68
Day 15 - It's Not Gonna Happen 72

Day 16 - Desperate People Dig Ditches.. *77*
Day 17 - Stay on Course.. *82*
Day 18 - Get Behind Me, Satan!... *87*
Day 19 - Be Angry and Sin Not.. *92*
Day 20 - God Always Has a Strategy... *97*
Day 21 - Lead By Example.. *102*

Finish Strong

Day 22 - It's Time to Break the Cycle.. *108*
Day 23 - I Can Do This!... *113*
Day 24 - Fight Like a Man.. *118*
Day 25 - Make the Most of Time... *123*
Day 26 - From Glory to Glory... *128*
Day 27 - Don't You Dare Give Up!.. *133*
Day 28 - Don't Fool Yourself... *138*
Day 29 - Power for Living *143*
Day 30 - Focus on the Mission.. *148*
Day 31 - Finish Strong... *153*

SECTION ONE:

Catch The Vision

Day 01

Use Your Imagination

"Now faith is the substance of things hoped for, the evidence of things we cannot see." ~ Hebrews 11:1

Imagination. That's a word often associated with childish fantasies, imaginary friends and that sort of thing—but we all have one. And, you know what? It's a great thing!

Faith and imagination go together. The Bible tells us in Hebrews 11:1 that "faith is the substance of things hoped for, the evidence of things we cannot see." We perceive the world through faith and imagination. That's what is meant by the biblical concept of "the eyes of faith"–imagining things that you cannot see; believing it before it is manifested.

So, what is imagination? Simply put, it's the ability to form new ideas, images or concepts of things not present to the senses at this particular time. The biblical concept also involves conception, meditation and muttering. Joshua 1:9 says, "the law shall not depart from your mouth, but you shall meditate upon it day and night." That word translated "meditate" means to mutter, to speak and re-speak; to take the thoughts and the words of God and not only think about them, but speak them.

Use Your Imagination

Imagination is important for another reason: It allows you to either live in fear or in faith. I choose to live in faith, and I hope you will too! Both fear and faith flourish through our imaginations. But as believers, we can imagine on a totally different level. 1 Corinthians 2:16 says, "We have the mind of Christ...and do hold the thoughts, the feelings, the purposes of His heart." Your imagination doesn't have to be earthly, carnal or fleshly: it can be heavenly!

I want you to rediscover your imaginative self. At one time in your life you were creative, but somehow you stopped imagining, stopped believing, stopped creating. Stir up your imagination once again! Stretch it further than you thought possible!

1 Corinthians 2:9-10 says, "Eye has not seen nor ear heard nor has it entered into the heart of man the things which God has prepared for those who love Him." Too often we stop right there, but you need to keep reading: "But God has revealed them to us through His Spirit. The Spirit searches all things, yes, the deep things of God." Verse 12 says, "Now we have received not the spirit of this world, but the Spirit who is from God that we may know the things that have been freely given to us by God."

God, through the Holy Spirit, wants us to excel in the area of imagination—to conceive, to believe and to act upon what God places in our hearts. That's pretty powerful, isn't it? God wants us to soar, to do what we've not done before. He wants us to use our faith, not just talk about faith. If we can believe and imagine that prayer works, then we should be praying. It's one thing to talk about prayer, but it's another to actually pray and believe that God's ears are attentive to the cries of His children.

God wants us to believe like we've never believed before, to imagine even though it seems like 1,000 doors have closed in front of you. It's not time for you to quit. It's time for you to go to the next door, because eventually the door is going to open. Here are a couple of declarations that I hope you will begin to make. Imagine these, if you will:

1. From this moment on, I will succeed: Defeat is not an option!
2. From this moment on, I will live and not die.
3. From this moment on, I am prosperous—not "broke, busted and disgusted," but blessed and highly favored of the Lord.
4. From this moment on, I am healed by His stripes.

Let the devil know you mean business! Someone once said, "The Stone Age didn't end because they ran out of stones." Think about that. Somebody used his imagination and moved us into another era. Walt Disney said, "It's kind of fun to do the impossible!" I like that! Stir your imagination. Do something the devil said you would never do because you can't afford it or you're the wrong gender or skin color. Defy the odds in Jesus' name and imagine that you can be successful at it!

But—here's the catch—in order for you or me to get to this place, we've got to be processed. Romans 12:1-2 says, "With eyes wide open to the mercies of God, I beg you, my brothers, as an act of intelligent worship, to give Him your bodies as a living sacrifice, consecrated to Him and acceptable by Him. Don't let the world around you squeeze you into its own mold, but let God remold your minds from within, so that you may prove in practice that the plan of God for you is good, meets all His demands and moves toward the goal of true maturity" (J.B. Phillips translation).

Your mind and imagination have been completely liberated through what Jesus Christ accomplished for you at Calvary. God wants you to remove the self-imposed limitations that have been holding you back and to present yourself to Him as holy—*transformed* rather than *conformed*.

Furthermore, with this renewed mind, you've got to have vision. Proverbs 23:7 says, "As a man thinks in his heart, so is he." Remember when the spies went out to survey the land? Ten came back with a negative report: "We were like grasshoppers." The giants who inhabited the land were so tall they felt like grasshoppers in comparison. It's time to open your eyes and see who and what God sees, to look past the giants and see the possibilities.

Beware these imagination killers: small-mindedness, complacency, and doubt (unbelief). Here's the type of thinking that happens when we let these three in:

Charles H. Duell, Commissioner of the U.S. Patent and Trademark Office said in 1899, "Everything that can be invented has been invented."

Grover Cleveland, in 1905, said, "Sensible and responsible women do not want to vote."

Lord Kelvin, President of the Royal Society in 1895 said, "Heavier-than-air flying machines are impossible."

The president of Michigan Savings Bank, while advising against investing in the Ford Motor Company, said, "The horse is here today, but the automobile is only a novelty, a fad."

Darrell Zannuck of Twentieth Century Fox, commenting on television in 1946, said, "People will soon get tired of staring at a plywood box every night."

Instead, think like this:

William Arthur Ward said, "Nothing limits achievement like small thinking. Nothing expands possibilities like unleashed imagination."

Antoine de Saint-Exupery said, "If you want to build a boat, do not instruct the men to saw wood, stitch the sails, prepare the tools and organize the work, but make them long for setting sail and travel to distant lands." In other words, if you have the desire, you will imagine how to get there.

Remember, Scripture says, "It is God who gives us to will and to do of His good pleasure" (Philippians 2:13). God will put the desire—and the imagination—there. And then He will give you the wherewithal to see that imagination come to fruition. Use your imagination today for God's glory! Anything is possible to those who believe!

Think It Through

What is imagination? _____
_____
_____

Why is imagination important? _____
_____
_____

What does it mean to meditate? _____
_____
_____

What "imagination killers" exist in your life? _____
_____
_____

List some ways you can better use your imagination: _____
_____
_____

Day 02
Greater is He in You

"You are of God, little children, and have overcome them, because He who is in you is greater than he who is in the world." ~ 1 John 4:4

Nestled into the ancient text of 1 John is a powerful kingdom principle for believers to remember. By this principle we should live our lives, conduct our affairs and minister in the name of Jesus. It is found in 1 John 4:4: "Greater is He that is in you than he that is in the world." The verse actually begins, "You are of God, little children…" That is emphatic: *You are a child of God!* Friend, it is very important that you know who you are. If you don't, then you will live far beneath your potential. If you don't know who you are, then it is likely you will live like you're somebody else. One old man put it this way: "Be who you is and not who you ain't, 'cause if you is who you ain't, then you ain't who you is!" You have got to know who you are—in God and in Christ. Otherwise, Satan will try to keep you from this kingdom principle, make you think you're weak and a loser. You're not a loser; you're a winner!

The scripture says, "You are of God and have overcome them." Overcome whom? The Antichrist and the spirit of Antichrist that is in the world. We know from such words as "antiperspirant" that the prefix "anti" mean that which is against, or that which is opposed to. So "antichrist" means that which opposes Christ, that which is against Christ. So this "spirit of Antichrist" is Satan himself, the demonic realm, the demonic agenda—not just the Antichrist personified in the End Times teachings.

The spirit of Antichrist will try to deceive you and lead you astray, but good news: You are an overcomer! Knowing that, you must remember that you have a treasure in an earthen vessel. Your outward man is perishing, according to Scripture, but the inward man is being renewed day by day. Your body is not perfect. It ages (don't we know it!). It's good to reflect upon the fact that what's most important is not who you are in the flesh (your college degree, work status, or how fit and wonderful your body may seem at the moment); what's most important is who you are in the spirit!

John, in his epistle, makes it very clear why you are an overcomer: Because "greater is He that is in you, than he that is in the world." Without Jesus in us, there is no overcoming. You can get your focus off you—and off what's in the world—and get it onto "the Big He," God Almighty, the One who is greater in you!

I said earlier that it's important to know who you are, and that's true. But it's also extremely important that you know who God is. How big is your God? How great is He?

The Bible tells us many things about God: He is a self-revealing God. From the opening statement in the book of Genesis, He reveals His nature to man: "In the beginning, God…" The Hebrew word is *Elohim*, the Creator God, the self-existent, eternal and righteous God. If we saw God for who He is, we wouldn't get so discouraged by the evil and godlessness of our culture. If we could keep the greatness of God before our eyes, we'd be gripped by His awesome reality. Just like it says in 2 Corinthians 3:18, When we see the greatness of God, we will be changed from one degree of glory to the next.

God is omnipotent (all-powerful, almighty), omnipresent (everywhere present), and omniscient (all-knowing). He is eternal, self-existent. God is self-sufficient (He doesn't need anybody else). God is transcendent, beyond our ability to describe or fully comprehend. But although He is transcendent, He is also imminent (present with us). God is sovereign. God is salvation and God is love. He is holy and just. And He is righteous. God is good, and His mercy endures forever. God is faithful even when we are unfaithful. God is our helper ("a very real and present help in times of trouble"). He is Jehovah Rapha (the God who heals us). And He is our deliverer. God is also a miracle-worker. And He is immutable (He never changes).

God is still on the throne. The only way Satan will ever be able to defeat you is if you are ignorant of who you are in Christ. If you don't know who you are in Christ, Satan will use his arsenal to try to keep you from that knowledge. Because if you know—really know—that the Greater One is inside of you, then defeat is not an option!

Evict the lies of the enemy from your life: discouragement, unbelief, poverty, sickness—tell them to leave in Jesus' name! Be of good courage, lift up your head and get back to doing what God has called you to do. Greater is He that is in you, than he that is in the world!

Think It Through

Explain what it means to be "of God": _____
_____
_____

What does it mean to be an overcomer? _____
_____
_____

List some of the attributes that describe the greatness of God: _____
_____
_____

List some lies of the enemy that you can evict from your life because you are a child of God: _____
_____
_____

Day 03

The Voice of the Lord

"My sheep hear My voice, and I know them, and they follow Me."
~ John 10:27

God still speaks to man, and you and I can know His voice: "I am the good shepherd and I know My sheep, and am known by My own. As the Father knows Me, even so I know the Father; and I lay down My life for the sheep. And other sheep I have which are not of this fold; them also I must bring, and they will hear My voice; and there will be one flock and one shepherd…My sheep hear My voice, and I know them, and they follow Me" (John 10:14-16, 27).

God reveals His will to us by His spoken word. He wants every one of us to hear His word because He wants all of us to know His will. Ephesians 5:15-17 says, "See then that you walk circumspectly, not as fools but as wise, redeeming the time, because the days are evil. Therefore, do not be unwise…" Let me stop here and share something with you: Years ago, I looked up the Greek word for "unwise" and it said "stupid." So, basically, God is warning us, "Don't be stupid…but understand what the will of the Lord is." If I don't understand what the will of the Lord is, I'm stupid; I'm unwise, according to the Scriptures—especially since the Word of the Lord is accessible and understandable.

Another reason God speaks to us is that He wants us to be found in the very center of His will. I encourage you not to make any major decisions without getting the will of God on them. In order to do this, you have to hear His word concerning it. Don't take a new job because it pays better than what you're making right now. For all you know that position may be phased out in six months. And please don't get married without asking the Lord, "Is this the one?" You can know the will of God for your life, but you need to listen to His voice to hear it.

God speaks. He's not mute like the idols of various religions around the world. But, the truth is, sometimes we mute Him. Sometimes God is speaking, but we've got the mute button on. Do yourself a favor: Don't turn a deaf ear to the voice of the Lord when He's speaking to you. We are so privileged to serve the true and living God. When we cry out to Him, He hears us, answers us, helps us, heals us, and delivers us from every one of our distresses. Hallelujah, He's a prayer-hearing, prayer-answering God!

Jesus promised that God will continue to speak to us through the coming of His Holy Spirit. John 16:12-14 says, "I still have many things to say to you, but you cannot bear them now. However, when He, the Spirit of truth, has come, He will guide you into all truth; for He will not speak on His own authority, but whatever He hears He will speak; and He will tell you things to come. He will glorify Me, for He will take of what is Mine and declare it to you."

I grew up hearing the saints talk about how God spoke to them, and honestly, I'm not sure if everything they said was really from God. It might have been that late-night pizza! But people said it in a way that you could tell they were familiar with the concept of hearing God's voice. When I came to know Jesus, I wanted to hear what they heard. I wanted to hear the voice of God. So when somebody said that God spoke to him, I'd wonder to myself, *Well, what does God sound like?* Was it audible, because when somebody talks to me, it's spoken aloud? So I just assumed that when God spoke, it was in an audible voice. Now, I'm sure you know that if God wants to, He can certainly speak in an audible voice. But let me warn you right here: don't you go seeking for that audible voice! You might hear some voices, but it might not be the voice of God. If He chooses to speak to you audibly, then so be it. He determines how He will communicate with you. The important thing is He will speak to you, through His Word, through the Holy Spirit, and you can expect to hear clearly what He has to say.

Acts 13:2 gives us an example of how God spoke to the early church: "As they ministered to the Lord and fasted, the Holy Spirit said, 'Now separate to Me Barnabas and Saul for the work to which I have called them.' Then, having fasted and prayed, they laid hands on them and they sent them away." What were they doing when the Holy Spirit spoke to them? They were in prayer, praising and worshiping the Lord. And in that atmosphere, the Holy Spirit spoke. If we're going to be a people who hear the voice of God, we've got to be a praying, worshiping people. That's one of the reasons the enemy doesn't want us to praise and worship the Lord: because he knows that when we get together in one accord and worship God, He will speak. If you need direction, guidance or help, then spend some time ministering to the Lord.

And keep those spiritual ears open so you can hear what God will say to you. It may be just a word or a paragraph; it may come in a dream. But know this: He will speak to you. Why? Because God wants to encourage you to trust Him and His Word, to know the sound of His voice. As you experience the fulfillment of His word, He knows your faith will grow strong, for faith comes by hearing and hearing by the Word of God. He will direct you in your decisions and order your steps, so you can experience what He has for you. But your ears have got to be open to the sound of His voice.

Matthew 7:24-27 says, "Therefore whoever hears these sayings of Mine, and does them, I will liken him to a wise man who built his house on the rock: and the rain descended, the floods came, and the winds blew and beat on that house; and it did not fall, for it was founded on the rock. But everyone who hears these sayings of Mine, and does not do them, will be like a foolish man who built his house on the sand: and the rain descended, the floods came, and the winds blew and beat on that house; and it fell. And great was its fall."

When it comes to listening, are you a fool or are you wise? I don't want you to forget that question because it's not just hearing His Word that matters; it's doing His Word. Hear the Word of the Lord, and then do the Word of the Lord, amen?

Think It Through

According to Matthew 4:4, what do we need, even more than physical sustenance, to live and why? _____
_____
_____

Why does God want us to hear His voce? _____
_____
_____

In what ways does God speak to His people? _____
_____
_____

Give an example of how God has spoken to you personally: _____
_____
_____

How can you apply Matthew 7:24-27 in your life? _____
_____
_____

Day 04

Dreams Really Do Come True

"And it shall come to pass afterward that I shall pour out My Spirit on all flesh. Your sons and your daughters shall prophesy, your old men shall dream dreams, your young men shall see visions." ~ Joel 2:28

Did you know that Joel 2:28 is the same passage Peter used on the Day of Pentecost? God gave him insight while he was preaching, proclaiming the gospel of Jesus Christ that pivotal day in church history. Peter, by the unction of the Holy Spirit, said we are living in that time when God says, "I am going to pour out My Spirit upon all flesh"—upon everybody who calls upon the name of the Lord. And then He says there are going to be dreams and visions.

You can expect to have dreams and visions. I don't care how old you are, I promise you that what's inside of you is greater than you know. If God left you here on this planet, He left you for a reason, and I think we need to start speaking to the greatness that's inside of us to the potential that is yet to be released, and we need to pull it out. We need to give it expression. Never underestimate the power of dreams. God speaks through dreams, and He reveals things to us through those dreams.

We can discern four types of dreams recorded around the time of Jesus' birth:

1. **Dreams of Assurance**:

Matthew 1: 20: "But while he thought about those things, an Angel of the Lord appeared to him in a dream, saying, "Joseph, son of David, do not be afraid to take unto you Mary as your wife, for that which is conceived in her is from the Holy Spirit." This dream is what we call the *Dream of Assurance*. Imagine Joseph, receiving the news that his bride-to-be is pregnant. Now imagine his emotional state: His world has just been turned upside down. But in the moment of his understandable despair, God gave him a *Dream of Assurance*. An angel appeared to him in that dream and said, "Now Joseph, don't be ashamed to take Mary as your wife." As a result of that dream, he went from despair that could possibly have led him to reject Mary, to being the earthly father of Jesus! God will give us dreams that bring us assurance. On many occasions, God has shared with me dreams that helped me to identify with what He was doing. God will give you dreams in the same way that will comfort and help you so that you, too, can discover what He is doing in your life. Maybe you're facing some challenges this year. Maybe you're feeling shattered or rejected due to some prevailing circumstance in your life. Well, there's good news for you! Be encouraged! Just as God gave Joseph a dream that put His stamp of approval upon what He was doing in his life, God will send us *Dreams of Assurance* to strengthen and encourage us as well!

2. **Dreams of Warning**:

Matthew 2:12-13: "Then, being divinely warned in a dream that they should not return to Herod, they departed for their own country another way. Now when they had departed, behold, an angel of the Lord appeared to Joseph in a dream, saying, 'Arise, take the young Child and His mother, flee to Egypt and stay there until I bring you word, for Herod will seek the young Child to destroy Him.'" Sometimes God communicates with us through *Dreams of Warning*. You've got to understand that there's a dream language, that things in dreams may be symbolic: colors, persons, occupations; if you're on a plane or a bus or in a car, a house or a bathtub. These dream images often represent entirely different things in the waking world. If you are going to do a Google search to try to figure it out, let me caution you to do a proper search for dream interpretations or symbols: type "Christian" in there, because there is a lot of New Age stuff on the internet, and that will take you somewhere you don't need to go. When God gives you a *Dream of Warning*, it might be that He is trying to re-route you or prevent you from coming under attack. Listen to the voice of the Holy Spirit.

3. **Dreams of Guidance**:

Matthew 2:19: "Now when Herod was dead, behold, an angel of the Lord appeared in a dream to Joseph in Egypt, saying, 'Arise, take the young Child and His mother and get to the land of Israel. For those who sought the young Child's life are dead.' And then he rose, took the young Child and His mother and went into the land of Israel." When they got to Israel, they were led by dreams to Nazareth to fulfill the prophecy, "And He shall be called a Nazarene." This kind of dream is a *Dream of Guidance*. God orders our steps. He will show you dreams and visions that signify where He is leading you. We all need guidance from the Lord, don't we? Why insist upon doing it your own way when you could save yourself some heartache, some money, and some pain? Trust the Lord. The Bible says, "Acknowledge the Lord in all your ways." He will give you dreams and visions as you face whatever comes your way this year. We need guidance as individuals, as families, and as churches.

4. **Dreams of the Miraculous**:

Luke 1:7,13: Another miraculous birth happened around the time of Jesus' birth: the announcement of the pregnancy of Elizabeth, who was barren and old. Then there was the angelic visitation that led to the birth of John. And finally, the miraculous birth of the Lord Jesus. These scriptures show us *Dreams and Visions of the Miraculous*. So many people are in need of miracles today.

God reminds us that, even with the story of the birth of the Lord Jesus Christ, miracles do happen. Let us not forget that the birth of Jesus was a miraculous gift from God to the entire world. I call Jesus "God's Love Gift to the World," not just to you and me but also to the world.

My friend, this is your time for miracles! Ask big. Expect big. And receive big, in Jesus' name! The day of miracles is not past because the God of Miracles is still present!

Whatever you need, if it's a Dream of Assurance, Warning, Guidance or Miracle, just keep your eyes on Jesus! He will direct your path.

Think It Through

According to Joel 2:28, what will happen when God's Spirit is poured out upon all flesh? _____
_____
_____

Has God spoken to you in a dream? If so, which of the four types listed was it and how did it help? _____
_____
_____

Why does God speak to us through dreams and visions? _____
_____
_____
_____

List another Biblical example of God speaking through a dream or vision:
_____
_____
_____

How can you be sure your dreams or visions are coming from God? ____
_____
_____
_____

Day 05

Decisions Determine Destiny

"I call heaven and earth as witnesses today against you, that I have set before you life and death, blessing and cursing; therefore choose life, that both you and your descendants may live." ~ Deuteronomy 30:19

Sometimes as we think about the destiny God has designed for us, we find the probability of that destiny in our future slim to none. We remember how we've missed opportunities or made poor choices; we see the consequences we've rightly deserved and believe that we may never come to the good end once envisioned for us. While God's will may include many course corrections for us, it is still attainable.

Your history, up to this point, is not your destiny. Your destiny is a matter of choice. This is why it is important to note that the choices you make today need to be the ones you can live with tomorrow.

There is this idea in the world that fate or destiny is a pre-determined course of events beyond human control. The typical response to such a belief is resignation: if we can't change destiny, then why should we even try? Whatever happens, happens; we can't do anything about it. This is called fatalism, and it is not biblical. You and I have been given the gift of choice. Our decisions determine our destiny. I love this quote by Roy

Disney: "It's not hard to make decisions when you know what your values are."

There are five things that the Lord impressed on me to share with you regarding values that will help you make the best decisions. These will lead you to success and not failure.

Be selective in the company you keep. This may sound harsh, but beginning now, get stupid people out of your life. The Bible says in 1 Corinthians 15:33, "Do not be deceived: Evil company corrupts good habits." It is important that you watch who you associate with. If you walk with wise men, you'll become wise. If you hang around fools, you'll be destroyed (Proverbs 13:20). The Message Bible says you'll "watch your life fall to pieces."

Guard your heart and mind. Proverbs 4:23 says, "Keep your heart with all diligence, for out of it spring the issues of life." Over and over in Scripture we are educated and warned that our hearts and minds are the incubator of our decisions. "As a man thinks in his heart, so is he" (Proverbs 23:7). Your destiny will reflect your inner thoughts. "Therefore," Peter instructs us, "Gird up the loins of your mind, be sober, and rest your hope fully upon the grace that is to be brought to you at the revelation of Jesus Christ " (1 Peter 1:13).

Watch your mouth. "Out of the abundance of the heart, the mouth speaks" (Luke 6:45). The decisions you make determine your destiny. Unfortunately, because we aren't guarding our hearts and minds, any and everything comes out of our mouths, tainting the favorable end God has designed for us. Proverbs 6:2 says that we are snared by the words of our mouths. Make sure you watch your mouth. Wake up with praise, speaking positivity, commanding your morning to cooperate and line up with the will of God. Stop speaking negatively. Stop speaking death over you and your family, your marriage, etc. Speak life!

Stop with the excuses. Check yourself. Make sure you're not being lazy (Proverbs 22:13). Make sure you're not spouting off excuses like those invited to the great supper in Luke 14:16-24. Understand that if you are, you'll be overlooked–not because God wants to overlook you, but because your decision to excuse yourself determines your destiny.

Be faithful in doing good. You don't want to have come all this way to quit now. "No one, having put his hand to the plow, and looking back, is fit for the kingdom of God" (Luke 9:62). Up till now, you've given talent, time, treasure. You've cast your bread upon the water–even in the most challenging of situations. I want to encourage you: what a man sows, that will he reap (Galatians 6:7). So do not "grow weary while doing good, for in due season we shall reap if we do not lose heart" (verse 9).

Look at God, beloved! He's made the psalmist's words come to pass in your life thus far! "I've never seen the righteous forsaken, nor his seed begging bread" (Psalm 37:25). I promise you every time you've cast bread upon the water, God has seen it and He will make good on His promise. He will cause the harvest, the blessing, the miracle, the healing you need to overwhelm you. I believe that in the heavenlies there are some things being sped up and released. The enemy's hand is bound and death is rebuked over you, in the name of Jesus. Peace is coming to rest upon you.

Remember, even with the challenges, frustrations, disappointments and losses of life, God has been with you. He's provided in the midst of it all. Thank Him for it! Like the psalmist, say, "I would have lost heart, unless I had believed that I would see the goodness of the Lord in the land of the living" (Psalm 27:13).

Pray this prayer: Thank you, Lord, for being merciful and loving me, for not letting me go. Thank You that You kept me in line when I was going astray. Thank You for the good work You've begun in me and Your commitment to its completion. Thank You for every answered prayer, for the opportunities I've enjoyed and the encounters in which I came to know

You in a new way. Bless me, speak peace to me, and prosper my soul. Thank You for my job, for success in line with your Holy Spirit. May Your glory rest upon me and Your angels encamp round about all that is mine. In Jesus' mighty name.

Think It Through

Is destiny "chance" or "choice"? Explain your answer: _____
_____
_____

Which of the five decision-making points do you need to work on? _____
_____
_____

In what ways can you re-shape your destiny through better decision-making? _____
_____
_____

How can God's promises help you make better life decisions? _____
_____
_____

List ways that God's promises encourage you, even during the tough times: _____
_____
_____

Day 06

There's a Treasure in You

"But we have this treasure in earthen vessels, that the excellence of the power may be of God and not of us." ~ 2 Corinthians 4:7

There is a great need for encouragers in the world today. While there is no shortage of discouragers, it is not as easy to find men and women who know how to lift broken spirits and give hope to those facing difficulties. I believe everyone is called to lift others with a positive and truth-filled word. Find a place to encourage people and your worth will skyrocket!

You are special. In today's contemporary usage of the word "special," it can mean a few things: precious, intriguing, valuable. It can also mean "special" like "one clown away from a circus," though, so let me specify. You, my friend, are far more valuable than you can imagine.

You are a treasure. A treasure is that which is good, valuable and precious. Treasure is often collected in a treasury or in particular packaging like a treasure chest. In our text, Paul said we have a treasure in earthen vessels. This terminology refers to clay jars. In antiquity, it was not uncommon to store valuable items in clay jars. You don't put precious things in junk. When a man wants to propose to a lady, he doesn't give her a diamond engagement ring in a Ziploc bag. It's too valuable for that! He displays it in a nice package. Such is the case with us. We are earthen vessels with a treasure inside. The implication is that we are fragile. Whether we admit it or not, we all have frailties. I know there are many people running around with big "S's" on their chests, but there's really not a Superman or Wonder Woman among us.

You are the apple of God's eye. I want you to see what God thinks about you. In Zechariah 2:8, the Lord of Hosts said, "He sent me after glory, to the nations which plunder you, for he who touches you touches the apple of His eye." You are the apple of His eye. I did a little research on this. The apple is the centermost part of the eye. It is the pupil. It is a very protected part because it is the most tender and useful part.

I learned as well that if you were close enough to look into the apple of someone's eye, you'd notice there's a reflection of you there. When God is looking at you, He expects to see a reflection of Himself. God wants to see Himself in you. I love that!

You are His portion. Deuteronomy 32:9-10 tells us that the Lord's portion is His people, His inheritance. You are not your own. You were bought with a price. You belong to God, therefore, honor God not just with your spirit, but with your body. I'm telling you, when you consider what God has done for you, it should keep a continuous praise welling up in you always.

You are an intentional creation. Right from the start, we can see how very special we are. God as Creator did nothing by accident. He was intentionally involved in every act of creation. Yet nothing we see in this life - majestic mountains, vast oceans, the distant stars - absolutely nothing compares to the summit of His creation: mankind. Nothing can touch mankind. By design, man is made in the image and likeness of God. You look like God. I don't mean in physical appearance. God is a spirit, and we are created in His image. We have spirit, soul and body. We are created as a representation of God here on earth. As His representations, we were given purpose and dominion.

You are God's partner. God created man not just for fellowship, but also for partnership. The heavens belong to the Lord, but He's given man the earth (Psalm 115:16), the beasts of the field, the birds of the air, the fish of the sea and everything that creeps on the earth (Genesis 1:28). God raised us up and gave us dominion, power and authority over everything on the earth. Now, because of the fall of man, everything is out of whack. We should never see a person running from a little spider! These little things have now taken a place because we've been *dis*placed. In God's original plan, we were given purpose and dominion. We were given creative ability, vision, intuition and intelligence.

You are what you think. Proverbs 23:7 says, "As a man thinks in his heart, so is he." If you think you're stupid, you'll act stupid. If you think you can't control your hormones, you won't control your hormones. If you think you'll never get ahead, you won't get ahead. If you think you can make it, then you will make it. If you think you're valuable, you'll take care of yourself as something valuable. If you think you can be victorious, then you'll be victorious! Lord, open my friend's eyes! God help us see who we really are!

Meditate on Deuteronomy 7. Consider what it says. You are holy, chosen, a special treasure. God has His sights set on you. You are part of a chosen generation and a royal priesthood (1 Peter 2: 9-10). The KJV calls you a "peculiar people." That simply means that you belong to God and are very special to Him. You may feel like the least of all. You may have suffered rejection and struggle with self-esteem, but don't allow that to translate over to your walk with God. He loves you. He accepts you. You are of incomparable value to Him. It's time to receive God's forgiveness for your failures. It's time to forgive yourself. I'm praying God gives you a release right now. The grace of Jesus is here for you. I'm believing that He will cleanse and remove from you anything that hinders you from living the way He designed you to live. Embrace His view of who you are and leave the thoughts of the world behind. As you do, I know He will complete His perfect work in you and cause you to live a fulfilling and rewarding life.

Think It Through

Why are you so important to God? List the reasons: _____
_____
_____

How are you an "earthen vessel with a treasure inside"? _____
_____
_____

List the "treasures" you carry within you: _____
_____
_____

How does negative thinking affect who you are? _____
_____
_____

Like David, you should encourage yourself in the Lord. What are some ways in which you can do this? _____
_____
_____

Day 07

The Invitation Still Stands

"Come now, and let us reason together... Though your sins are like scarlet, they shall be as white as snow." ~ Isaiah 1:18

I've seen a whole lot in ministry over the years. Rarely does a day go by that I am not fully engaged in trying to help up another fallen soldier, someone who's wrestling with a problem. I believe Jude 24, that God is able to keep you from falling. Still I know that whenever people take their eyes off Jesus, they begin to sink, just as Peter sank. The Lord delivered Peter when he lost focus, and I know that He will deliver each of us as we reaffix our eyes upon Him.

God's grace is sufficient. It is more than enough. This gift that is free to us does not come cheap. This is why I believe grace must not be perverted, twisted, distorted or undervalued. Some approach the message of grace with a cavalier attitude. Please understand grace is never a license for sinful living. Don't think God winks at sin. It's not that way. Paul said, "God forbid! How can we who are dead to sin live in it?"

Grace cooperates with God. Grace works *with* God because it works *for* God. Grace teaches, as we read in Titus 2:11, that "...we should live self-controlled, upright and godly lives in this present age." The grace of

The Invitation Still Stands

God operating in you will cause you to walk in ways that are congruent with the ways of the Holy Spirit. It will teach you to love, be merciful, and suffer long. It will lead you in a direction that brings the Lord pleasure and praise, rather than grieve His Holy Spirit. Keep this in mind. You should be grateful for God's grace, that when you blow it, He extends it toward you.

The message of grace does not inspire me to keep doing my own thing. No! That's a dangerous perspective to have! I feel inspired, like Isaiah who saw the Lord's train fill the temple. The more he saw of Him, the more he saw of himself, that he was undone and dwelt among unclean people. When I see God, I see how I fall short. Isn't it good that He who knew no sin became sin for us, so we could become the righteousness of God? Now His love compels me to relate to others in a way that will please the Lord. How you can say you love God but hate and hurt your brother is beyond me! What a contradiction!

In Isaiah 1, God speaks to His people. They had messed up big time. He spoke of how He had nourished and brought up children, and they had rebelled, forsaking His ways and deserving the consequence of God's deaf ear. "Even though you make many prayers, I will not hear," He said in verse 15. Fortunately, He didn't stop there.

Whenever God points out a problem, He provides a solution. In verses 16-18, God said, "Wash yourselves, make yourselves clean; put away the evil of your doings from before My eyes. Cease to do evil, learn to do good; seek justice, rebuke the oppressor; defend the fatherless, plead for the widow. Come now, and let us reason together... Though your sins are like scarlet, they shall be as white as snow."

"Come now" is a divine invitation. He means NOW. God, fully aware of their sinful condition, was reaching out and calling them back to Himself. Israel was straddling both sides of the fence, but despite the depth of their wickedness, God offered grace and mercy. They had only to repent!

Despite your sinful condition, God is calling you the same way. The timing of your invitation is NOW, and there is no option to delay because tomorrow is not promised to you.

"Let us reason together," God said. In other words, "Let's take it to a court of law." God had just spent the first portion of this chapter stating His case, and now He encourages them to state their case, if they can. The invitation was not to debate, but an opportunity for them to acknowledge their sin and guilt, and to repent. God does not want His people to brush their sins under the rug. He wants us to deal with them because they are hindrances to His perfect will for our lives. He wants us to lay aside every sin and every weight that slows us down and entangles us.

He said, "Though your sins are like scarlet, though they are red as crimson..." The words "scarlet" and "crimson" refer to a dye that was extracted from both shellfish and a certain insect. The dye was so potent that whenever it was used to dye a white garment, the garment would never be white again. The colors were colorfast and indelible. It would require a miracle for the garments to revert to their original state of white. Try what we can and do what we will, nothing can wash us whiter than snow or cleanse us but the blood of Jesus. I'm so grateful for that blood!

No matter your condition, no matter how it looks. You might think you've done the worst thing that anyone could ever do, and that God will never receive you to Himself again. I want you to know that is a lie from the enemy, for the word of God is clear in 1 John 1:9, "If we confess our sins, He is faithful and just to forgive us our sins and cleanse us from all unrighteousness." God will not treat you as man would. He will not cast you aside, kick you to the curb, and throw you away like common trash. God is attentive to the cries of His children even when they mess up. He says, "I'll give you another chance."

God is the God of another chance. You may have blown it big time. You may have ruined your name. But God will reach down where you are and lift you up out of your mess. He won't keep it before you the rest of your life. He won't hold it against you. God will look beyond it to see your need. His grace is amazing!

You may not be perfect and you may stumble along the way, but God's love for you will never change. Nothing will make Him stop loving you. The enemy would like to convince you that when you've blown it, you can never be used in the Kingdom again. The devil is a liar. Oftentimes, when you mess up and then come to yourself, you're often in a better place to be compassionate to someone else.

As we read on in our passage, we see God end his conversation with this final thought. He says, "If you're willing and obedient, I will restore what you've lost" (verses 19-20). My friend, there's still hope! Though you might have messed up, remember your purpose. Regain your focus. Get back on track. God will not reject you.

Do you have areas that need improvement? Release them to God. Simply acknowledge to Him that you've missed it. Ask for forgiveness and thank Him for His love, grace and mercy. Thank Him for His Word that gives you life and light. You have hope in Christ Jesus! When you repent and turn from your sins, when you allow Him to perfect and strengthen what's weak and lacking in you, you bring Him great pleasure. Receive His forgiveness and move forward today. He has amazing things in store for you!

Think It Through

God's grace is sufficient. Explain what that means to you: _____
_____
_____

What does grace teach you? _____
_____
_____

What important truth does Isaiah teach us about God's grace? _____
_____
_____

What is the lie of the enemy that seeks to keep you from God's grace? ___
_____
_____

What can you do to keep your focus on God, so that you stay on track?
_____
_____
_____

Day 08

You Have Potential

"…That the God of our Lord Jesus Christ, the Father of glory, may give to you the spirit of wisdom and revelation in the knowledge of Him, 18 the eyes of your [a]understanding being enlightened…" ~ Ephesians 1: 17-18

There are many people living clueless upon this earth. Cemeteries are filled with once gifted but unfulfilled people. They never gave their ability responsibility. They did not recognize, release or reveal the capabilities God placed within them.

Paul's prayer in Ephesians 1:15-21 is a timeless prayer that reaches us in our contemporary day. His desire was for believers to receive the spirit of wisdom and revelation in the knowledge of God. Isaiah 33:6 clearly states that "wisdom and knowledge" is the stability of our times. Paul wanted us to know God's power, our calling and His inheritance.

You were born pregnant with incredible potential. What you've seen thus far in your life is just a glimpse of your capability. You are here at this time in history to address a specific need that you were created to meet. I promise you, you are not here to make things worse; you're here to make them better!

Just what is potential? It is *currently unrealized ability*. It is something capable of being, but latent, undeveloped and unreleased. All you've done thus far is just a scratch on the surface of what you can do, but because you've done it, it is no longer your potential.

God expects us to take what we've been given and be responsible for it. To that end, I've put together a list of the seven critical things you must do to fulfill your God-given potential:

1. Discover Your Purpose. Dr. Myles Munroe said, "Where purpose is not known, abuse is inevitable." If you don't know the purpose of a spouse, you'll abuse or undervalue that spouse. If you do not know your purpose, you'll abuse your time. Do you know some things take time? If you're sincere about discovering your purpose, you're going to have to draw it out (Proverbs 20:5). You may not know what gift is yours today, but if you will get before the Lord, you'll discover it! God is waiting to reveal it to you. You just have to choose to release it. How badly do you want it? I want it badly enough to make changes when they are necessary.

2. Deny Yourself, Take Up Your Cross and Follow Jesus. Too many people are stuck on self. It is only by total death to self that we can truly and completely live for Christ. Consider what Jesus said to His disciples in Matthew 16:24-26. You must surrender self-ambitions to God, pick up your cross daily, and keep your eyes on Jesus. Follow Him, not your own agenda!

3. Stay Connected to the True Vine and the Body of Jesus Christ. Jesus said in John 15:4-5, "For without Me you can do nothing." If you are going to release potential, your source of potential is God. If you ever get disconnected, you and your potential will die. Some people are clear on that. They say, "I'll go with Jesus all the way." But often, they don't stay connected to the body of believers with the same tenacity. They fall out of relationships too easily. They leave church over minor squabbles. If you find yourself in a situation where a brother or sister is getting on your nerves, don't ask God *why* you have to put up with him or her; ask God *what* He's trying to teach you through the experience!

4. Don't Limit God. Don't make the same mistake Israel did in limiting the Holy One (Psalm 78:41)! It was an insult! We've got too much work ahead of us, too many prophetic words, too many unctions, too many dreams and visions for us to limit the One who makes all things possible. Francis Chan well said, "If my mind is the size of a soda can and God is the size of all the oceans, it would be stupid for me to say He is only the small amount of water I can scoop into my little can." Take the limits off! With God, you can do far more than you can even consider! He is waiting to usher you into new realms!

5. Stir Up the Gift. Timothy became discouraged in his work. Paul said to him, "It's affected you. Your flame is flickering. I want you to remember your gifts and stir them up on the inside of you" (2 Timothy 1:6). It's not God's place to stir up your gift; it's yours! Some people allow their flame to wane because of injuries they sustain at the hands of others. I understand this temptation, but we must advance past the pain. Leo Buscaglia said, "Your talent is God's gift to you. What you do with it is your gift back to God."

6. Get Rid of Fear. Life is much too short to let fear make decisions for you, to cripple you, to hold you back. God hasn't given you this spirit. He's given you power, love and a sound mind, as we read in 2 Timothy 1:7. Eric Hoffer said, "You can discover what your enemy fears most by observing the means he uses to frighten you." Whatever the devil is trying to keep you from doing is most likely what God has for you to do! Work out your own salvation with fear and trembling. It is God Who gives us to will and to do according to His good pleasure.

7. Serve Others for God's Glory. Robert Ingersoll aptly said, "You will rise by lifting others." You have a gift that God expects you to be responsible for. He expects you will use it to serve others (1 Peter 4:10). If you're not already involved in volunteer work or ministry, get involved. You may not be able to give the same service or time as another, but you can give the same quality. There's something you can do that will enrich and grow the Body of Christ. Paul said every joint supplies. If you detach your hand from its arm, your hand has no supply. In this way, we need one another. We need to be involved so every joint can provide its supply.

Some people don't get very far in life, and that's because they're always doing "less than" rather than going the extra mile. If you're ever to find your potential, you must first find Christ. Wherever you're working, recognize that's your assignment. Be productive in your situation as if you are working for the Lord Jesus. And when you work, you will work out!

Think of something you want to achieve and imagine accomplishing it. You are positioned to receive special favor from God! If He gave you the dream, and you know you can't accomplish it without Him, then it's significant. It's probably a dream from God. If what you're pursuing does not require God, it's probably not from Him! Your potential is inseparable and absolutely linked to God's potential. I encourage you to roll up your sleeves and get back to business. Believe for great things. Do great things. Achieve great things!

Think It Through

What is "potential"? _____
_____
_____

What does it mean to be "pregnant with possibilities"? _____
_____
_____

What potential do you feel lies untapped within you? _____
_____
_____

Which of the seven points do you struggle with most? _____
_____
_____

What can you do today to release your potential? _____
_____
_____

Day 09

There Is a Way Out

"Do not be afraid. Stand still and see the salvation of the Lord, which He will accomplish for you today." ~ Exodus 14:13

Have you ever felt backed into a corner with no way out? Maybe it was in a physical "fight or flight" moment; maybe it was that feeling you get when circumstances begin to crowd around you. I know I have experienced those moments.

In Exodus 14, we find the Israelites experiencing the same. Their backs against the Red Sea, they watched their enemies, the Egyptian army, riding toward them with great speed and evil determination. Like in the movies, I find this the perfect moment to "press pause" and revisit the very beginning of the story that led them to this place of no escape.

Israel was not always in slavery to Egypt. When they first settled in the land, it was as honored guests and family members of Joseph, the reigning pharaoh's vizier. Thirty years and several leaders later, the new pharaoh recognized that Israel had become a great nation and posed a threat to his own people. Circumstances had changed. Something must be done. So he placed over them task masters and afflicted them with many burdens.

There Is a Way Out

For 400 years, the Israelites served their overlords. Then one day God said, "Enough. It's time for a transition, a breakthrough." He sent a deliverer in the form of a helpless baby who needed to be delivered himself (and it wasn't the last time He did so!). The infant was placed in a basket which floated downstream to the bathing pool of Egypt's princess. She took pity upon him and raised him as her own.

This child, Moses, grew to one day defend a fellow Jew, causing the death of an Egyptian. In fear, he fled to the wilderness until God spoke to Him from the burning bush. We all know the story. Plagues. Denied requests. Hardened hearts. Death of the firstborn. Israel was finally allowed to leave, and they took with them the wealth of their Egyptian neighbors.

Yet just a short time after they were freed, Pharaoh became bent on revenge, dogging the Israelites with his best chariots and horsemen. Fast forward to verses 13 and 14 of our text. We find God's people with their backs against the wall of the Red Sea. Despair gripped many as they could envision no positive outcome. Moses spoke to the people, saying, "Do not be afraid. Stand still and see the salvation of the Lord, which He will accomplish for you today…The Lord will fight for you, and you shall hold your peace."

I believe this story is critical to our understanding of God's plans. Whether you realize it or not, you have an enemy who has sought to enslave you. Many people don't notice this because they don't know who they are. They underestimate their talent, skill and anointing, failing to recognize that they are indeed a threat to the enemy. Yes, the threat of God's people is Satan's reality. 1 John 4:4 tells us that we are more powerful than we imagine because "greater is He that is within you than he that is in the world." The enemy has a better understanding of your position in Christ than you do! This is why he bombards your mind with lies. Don't allow him to walk all over you. Enough is enough!

Maybe today, as you're reading, you find yourself identifying with the

Israelites. Maybe you are in a place less than desirable, unsolicited, a place of oppression, enslavement or confinement. Maybe you, too, should say, "Enough is enough!"

God is never without an exit strategy. He is never without a promise for deliverance. There is always a way out. Just as God raised up Moses to be a deliverer and to fulfill His word, He will not let any word that comes out of His mouth return to Him void, unproductive or fruitless. If God has ever spoken a thing to you, you can count on it. If He's given you a promise, you can take it to the bank!

It's one thing to say we believe God, but real faith must stand trial. The Word of God is proven in our lives when we're under attack. If you hold onto it, allowing it to become part of your very being, you will not buckle under the pressure but stand in victory. All this drama is developing something inside of you to prepare you for your next level of living. It is incubating greatness! Although this time may have been unrequested and unwanted, you can rest confident that it will both accomplish a purpose and expire right on time.

The Bible tells us that after 400 years of slavery, the Lord heard the cries of His people. Child of God, there is a point when God's promises and processes come to their appointed time. We can all receive that God will give us a promise, but we often find it hard to receive the accompanying process. We don't like it! We especially don't like it if the process requires that we wait, because we are some of the most hurried people. We treat God the way we treat fast food employees: "Hurry up!" Yet, there are some things you simply have to wait on. You cannot hurry God. The good news is He is never late! Psalm 34:17-19 reminds us that God will deliver us out of ALL of our troubles, not just some.

God used a series of events to free His people. Finally, Pharaoh couldn't go on. He said, "Get these people out of my face." Satan is the same way. He doesn't want you free, but eventually he will say, "Get him or her out of my face." The Israelites walked out of their land with boldness. Yet no sooner had Pharaoh released Israel, then he desired to enslave them again. Your enemy is also relentless, but don't sweat it. It's just a set up. When God has a plan for you, nothing the enemy does, no weapon formed against you shall prosper. You must not be intimidated by his tactics. No matter what you find yourself facing today, Romans 8:28 is still in the Bible. *"All things work together for good to those who love God."*

The Israelites' backs were against the Red Sea. There was no visible way out. But my friend, there is always a way out. For them, it was *through* the sea on dry ground! Once through safely, the sea crashed down upon the Egyptians. I wonder, did it close to drown the enemies or to shut the door, so to say, so that the Israelites would have no way back when the journey in front of them became too hard?

I want to encourage you to find your freedom in Christ. When you do, don't go back. The Israelites were called into the wilderness to a place of freedom, where worship could go forth and God could move them into a land of promise. The devil, like Pharaoh, doesn't want you free to worship God. He wants to distract you, afflict you, steal from you and make you sick. Worship anyhow! When you do, "out of your belly shall flow rivers of living water" (John 7:38). What did Pharaoh's army die in? Water! They drowned in water. If you will but open your mouth and praise the Lord, I guarantee you'll drown your pharaoh, your enemies and your troubles! Just stand and watch God fight for you when you praise Him!

Think It Through

Describe a time when you felt as if your back was "up against the wall."
_____
_____
_____

How did God deliver you from that time? _____
_____
_____

"God is never without an exit strategy." Explain what this means to you:
_____
_____
_____

Why must real faith stand trial? _____
_____
_____

Explain how Romans 8:28 has worked in your life: _____
_____
_____

Day 10

This Is Your Day

"For this purpose the Son of God was manifested, that He might destroy the works of the devil." ~ 1 John 3:8

Do you know Jesus? If you know Jesus, you know the Truth! He is the Way, the Truth and the Life. In John 8:31-35, Jesus announces that the truth *you know* shall set you free. The enemy knows that the presence of God is transforming and the word that comes forth will be liberating. This is why he is so disruptive and distracting in your daily life. He wants to keep you away from the truth, away from freedom and change.

God has the best of intentions and the best of plans for you. His desire is that you be wholly free. When Jesus saves, He saves to the uttermost; He saves completely. 2 Corinthians 5:17 tells us, "If anyone is in Christ, he is a new creation; old things have passed away; behold, all things have become new." When I received Jesus into my heart, there was a new awareness, a new perspective. When you are saved, you undergo a mind-set change and an appetite change. If nothing's changed, you haven't been born again!

Today, I want you to recognize that God has plans for your freedom. I want to remind you of the "full package" purchased for you at Calvary.

Christ came to set you free in every way. Today, if you will but believe, is YOUR day to be released!

You are released! Why is that so important to understand? Because some people have been released, but they don't live like it. History tells us that when the American slaves were emancipated, many didn't get the news till some time after; and even then, they still chose to live as slaves. Similarly, we have the document of redemption signed, sealed and delivered, but we can still choose to live under the harsh oppression of an enemy who comes to steal, kill and destroy. Sometimes we struggle because we have not received a proper diet of Scripture (faith comes by hearing, as you know). Sometimes we don't go further than receiving Christ into our hearts, and thus we don't receive His liberty in other areas of our lives. I don't want you to live your life this way! I want you to *know* the truth that sets you free. I want you to walk as one released from the oppression of your enemy.

In Luke 13:10-17 we read the account of the woman with a spirit of infirmity. Verse 11 tells us that she was plagued with a spirit of infirmity for eighteen years. She was "bent over and could in no way raise herself up." Jesus called her to Him and said, "Woman, you are loosed from your infirmity." He laid hands on her and immediately she straightened and glorified God!

All of us know the pain of infirmity and affliction. We know what it's like to struggle with things in life. Her struggle lasted eighteen years. Some of us couldn't last eighteen weeks! This evil spirit rendered her bent over so that she couldn't raise herself up. It is implied that she tried to lift herself but couldn't. Have you ever been humanly unable to do anything about your situation?

When you're bent over, you're in a position you'd rather not be in. Your vision is impaired and your perspective is challenged. As time wears on, you can become discouraged and give up trying to straighten up! No doubt, like this woman, you'd get used to your condition. You'd learn to compensate; you'd learn survival skills. I've seen people in bad marriages do this–they learn how to go with it. They get to the place where they accept, "He's always been a player, and he always will be." Like this woman, they get to a place where they think, "This is all I have to look forward to: the ground." Then, one day you're in the right place at the right time...

The Bible says in verse 12 that Jesus saw her. God's eyes go to and fro across the earth. He sees us in our condition and He won't leave us there! Jesus called the woman to Himself. He could have walked over to her, but there are some things you need to do to make *your* move towards Jesus.

When the woman came, Jesus said, "Woman, you are *freed* from your oppression." He touched her, and immediately she straightened up. All you need is a word from the Lord, just one touch from Him, and it will change every condition of your life. Immediately! Remember: she had been in this condition for eighteen years. You'd think it would take weeks for her to stand up. You'd think there would be a longer process. But Scripture says, "Immediately she was straightened."

May I be real with you? It isn't going to take long. This is a word of immediacy for you. If you can just grasp it by faith, God will do a quick work in you!

What the Bible says next about the woman's behavior is telling. As soon as she straightened up, she glorified God. She did what was fitting to do! I imagine she leapt around, twirled, skipped. She didn't hold back. While she was doing so, the religious people were filled with indignation, and they started criticizing Jesus, "This is the Sabbath! You aren't supposed to do any work today!" Jesus said, "Really? If you had a donkey that was stuck in a ditch, wouldn't you let it go free on the Sabbath? This woman is a daughter of Abraham!"

Don't be surprised if not everyone rejoices with you as you rejoice in victory. Some people would rather see you remain bent over than straightened up. Don't worry about them; God will speak up for you. He will put your adversaries to shame, as He did hers. He will prepare a table for you in the presence of your enemies. He will arrange it, set you there, and show His favor.

It's good to notice that even in her bent over condition, this woman was recognized by God as a daughter of Abraham. Your condition won't rob you of your position unless you let it. I understand that you are in a process, and that process must be completed before you can truly be free. Just keep your eyes on Jesus. He sees every tear and knows your pain. If He allowed your current condition, it's not to harm you but to help you. As you *go through*, know that you'll *come through*. It might have been an eighteen-year wait, but you will have an immediate recovery!

Today, you might be bent over emotionally. Your mind may be fatigued. You might feel like a candidate for breakdown. You might be having anxiety or panic attacks. Never again! God is releasing you even now. Just receive it. Receive the freedom He brings to you. There might be an antagonizing enemy speaking suicide in your ear. Don't fall for the lie. The Lord is healing you now as you cry out to Him. He will deliver you. Remember that Jesus confirmed Luke 4:16-21. He said, "Today this scripture is fulfilled in your hearing." He acknowledged He was sent and anointed to heal the brokenhearted and liberate the oppressed. 1 John 3:8 tells us He came to destroy the works of the devil. You may be struggling. You might want to get out of your situation. Today is your day. Be saved! Be healed! Be delivered! You are released in the name of Jesus!

Think It Through

What is holding you down, keeping you from moving forward in Jesus?
_____
_____
_____

Why is it so important for you to know personally that you are released?
_____
_____
_____

What did the woman in Luke 13 do immediately after Jesus healed her?
_____
_____
_____

What does her reaction teach you about your reaction to God's healing work in your own life?_____
_____
_____

When trials come, how should you face them? _____
_____
_____

SECTION TWO:

GET MOVING

Day 11

If You'll Do This, Then I'll Do That

"And all these blessings shall come upon you and overtake you, because you obey the voice of the Lord your God." ~ Deuteronomy 28:2

Deuteronomy 28:1-14 is a powerful passage of scripture that deals with the blessings of God. Christians love to hang out in Deuteronomy 28, where it speaks of God's promised blessings to us. But we must keep this in mind: the blessings of God are contingent upon our obedience to the Lord. Notice the "ifs" of verses 1, 2, 9,13 and 14. Some things in life and in the kingdom will not happen until you meet the conditions.

If you do the Word (meeting the condition), then you can expect God to bless you, spirit, soul and body. We see the idea of sowing and reaping throughout the scriptures. For instance, if you want to have friends, then sow some friendly seed and take care of them, so they'll produce a harvest. If you want a happy home, you've got to sow some seeds for that. I'm going to give you seven things you can expect when you obey God:

You will eat the good of the land (Isaiah 1:19): Don't try to talk yourself out of a blessing. He said if you're willing and obedient—so *be* willing and obedient and you *will* eat the good of the land.

You will be exalted, if you humble yourself (Matthew 23:12): If you exalt yourself, you will be humbled, but if you humble yourself, you will be exalted. God resists the proud, but He gives grace to the humble. I want grace, don't you?

You will receive answers to prayer, if you have faith in God (Jeremiah 33:3): 'Call to Me, and I will answer you, and show you great and mighty things, which you do not know.' Some people would rather call anybody else than call God. Although I understand the human need to reach out to others, the fact is, people are limited. We are finite beings and can't do everything. But "with God all things are possible." He's the God of all flesh and there is nothing too hard for Him to do. Jesus said, "Whatever things you ask, when you pray, believe that you receive them, then you will have them." God says, "If you will take the time to pray, I will bless you."

You will never stumble or fall, if you add to your faith (2 Peter 1:5-11): "giving all diligence, add to your faith virtue, to virtue knowledge, to knowledge self-control, to self-control perseverance, to perseverance godliness, to godliness brotherly kindness, and to brotherly kindness love. For if these things are yours and abound, *you* will be neither barren nor unfruitful in the knowledge of our Lord Jesus Christ." If you make your calling and election sure, you will never stumble—*if you add to your faith*. If you make certain that you're being nurtured, if you're growing in grace and in the knowledge of your Lord and Savior Jesus Christ. If these conditions are met, then you will never be barren or unfruitful. And you'll never stumble or fall!

You will reap bountifully, if you give generously (Luke 6:38): Here, the context is giving love, mercy, and forgiveness. The context is not judging and condemning others. But it is a principle or law of the kingdom that if you give, it shall be given back to you "good measure, pressed down, shaken together and running over will be put into your bosom. For with the same measure that you use, it will be measured back to you." That same measure—with the same quality, sacrifice, and generosity—and even above and beyond, God said, "I will have men pour into you." When you give generously, then you take a key and insert it into a blessing door, and when the doors of God open, no man can shut them, amen? Paul said, "Those who give sparingly will reap sparingly, but those who sow bountifully will reap bountifully."

You will reap if you don't lose heart (Galatians 6:7-9): "Do not be deceived, God is not mocked; for whatever a man sows, that he will also reap. For he who sows to his flesh will of the flesh reap corruption, but he who sows to the Spirit will of the Spirit reap everlasting life. And let us not grow weary while doing good, for in due season we shall reap if we do not lose heart." This is not the hour, my friend, to faint or be weary. You are on the brink of a miracle, closer now than you have ever been before. All the seed that you have sown has come before the Lord your God and He says, "If you refuse to faint; if you refuse to be weary, if you don't quit God and walk away, you will reap!" But you cannot faint. God is not a man that He should lie. Psalm 126:5 says, "Those who sow in tears shall reap in joy," but you will "doubtless come again…bringing [your] sheaves with [you]." In other words, you may sow in sorrow, but you will reap in great joy!

You will be blessed when you bless the Lord (Psalm 103:1-5): If you praise the Lord at all times, you can expect amazing things to come into your life. Praise is not just something we do on a Sunday morning. It's not going through some mechanical expression. It is something that is truly of the heart. I put it this way: Praise and worship is not just something I do; it is who I am! Some people can only praise and worship on a Sunday morning at 11:00 in a church sanctuary. And others don't have to be in church. Wherever they are, all they have to do is think about God, think about salvation, think about His goodness and His presence, think about His love. All they have to do is reflect upon what God has already done–and before you know it, there's a stirring going on way down on the inside, the stirring of praise in which they get a bad case of the "Can't-

Help-Its!" And when that happens, you will praise God, come what may. You will praise the Lord at all times! The reason some people don't see blessings in their lives is due to the fact that they don't thank God for what He's already done for them! If you want more of God, then you have to praise Him more. If you want more blessings, then you have to praise Him more! When you praise Him, blessings come down, healings come down, and miracles happen, amen?

Friend, just remember this truth: *If you'll do this, then He'll do that!* What is it that you need Him to do? What is your "that"? Begin to praise Him for it and obey His Word, and you will see the blessings of the Lord descend upon you!

Think It Through

Simply put, what must you do to see the blessings of God in your life? __
_____
_____

Which of the seven points do you struggle with? _____
_____
_____

What do you think is the root of your struggle? _____
_____
_____

According to today's devotional, what is the answer? _____
_____
_____

What do you want God to do for you today? _____
_____
_____

Day 12

Five Things You Should Know on the Way Up

"Then, as He was now drawing near the descent of the Mount of Olives, the whole multitude of the disciples began to rejoice and praise God with a loud voice for all the mighty works they had seen." ~ Luke 19:37

Each one of us is on a journey up from somewhere, going somewhere. I'm going to share some helpful insights regarding things to consider while you're on your trip. These things will–if you'll pardon the pun–keep you from trippin', so that you may finish your journey victoriously. The five truths are found in Luke 19:28-40, which details Jesus' triumphal entry into Jerusalem.

1. **The way up is costly**. Jesus was heading to Jerusalem, fully aware that this trip would end in His death at Calvary. You and I aren't headed toward that kind of cross, but we each have our own cross to bear. And our experience on this journey called Life will have its own sacrifices, as well. Jesus got on the cross willingly, and it cost Him everything He had. If you are to walk this road and fulfill your purpose and destiny, it's going to be costly. It's going to cost you some so-called friends. You'll be lied to. And if you're doing something worthwhile on your way up, people are going to talk about you. Some people will stab you in the back. Betrayal is on this road, my friend! People will smile in your face and then, when your

back is turned, they will criticize you or hate on you. I'm just being real here; cost comes with territory. If Jesus went through it, then you're going to go through it. Keep your eyes on Jesus and be willing to have your own Garden of Gethsemane proclamation, "Nevertheless not my will, but Your will be done." The rewards far outweigh the price of sacrifice many times over. In the Kingdom, understand that the way *up* is *down*. If you want to go up in life, then you're going to have to come down. "He who exalts himself will be abased, but he who humbles himself will be exalted." That's the Word of the Lord.

2. **God loves to use ordinary things and ordinary people.** This second truth is found in the selection of the donkey. Jesus requested a donkey—a symbol of humility and servanthood—to ride during His triumphal entry into Jerusalem. So, what's the point? If He could find a donkey and use it, surely He can find you and me...and use us! You may think you're too ordinary, that you have nothing to offer. Congratulations! You're just the one He's been looking for! God wants somebody who's not stuck on himself. He's looking for somebody who'll say, "Lord, here I am: use me!" Let Him use you, then give Him the glory for the job done.

3. **On your way up, expect revelations of Jesus Christ**. You are journeying in the School of the Holy Spirit. God will take you to certain places and through certain classes. You've got to attend those classes. You can't tell God, "No, thanks, I'm opting out!" There are no electives! God will usher you into environments and circumstances to teach you what you need to know—about Himself...and about yourself. If you hunger and thirst for the Lord (and I hope you do!) eventually you're going to see something of Him that you've never seen before. He's going to reveal things to you—about life, about people, about yourself. You'll learn you're not flawless; you've got imperfections. I've had to learn that about myself. Honestly, I've got a lot of flaws. Now that doesn't mean I'm out there practicing sin. I'm just saying that if you catch me on the wrong day, tired and hungry, I may not be as pleasant as I am right now. God will allow certain experiences in your life to show you that if you're not mindful

to keep your flesh down, you can say some things that you might regret later. Or do some things that will be shameful—and you don't want to go there! Whatever God allows in your life is not meant to bring you down but to show you that you still have room to grow. And, along the way, Jesus will reveal Himself to you as your Comforter, Counselor, Deliverer, Healer, and so much more!

4. **Everybody shouting your praises is not your friend.** People started spreading their cloaks on the road as Jesus drew near, and the multitudes began shouting and rejoicing, praising God. People took palm branches, threw them in the streets and waved them. But some of the people shouting Jesus' praises that day were, later that week, shouting, "Crucify him!" When people are talking about you and saying how wonderful you are, don't take it seriously! Because people can celebrate you one day and hate you the next. Keep your eyes on Jesus. Don't be fooled by the praise of men.

5. **If you're going to make this journey and come out victoriously, then you've got to do so with praise**. The Pharisees disapproved of the praises to Jesus. They said, "You need to rebuke those people! They're calling you 'Messiah!' Tell them to shut up!" Jesus replied, "If these were to be silent, the very rocks would cry out!" Your journey must be one of praise. Along the way, you're going to meet some people who won't like your praising self. Keep on praising! I'm grateful I had the privilege of being taught about praising and magnifying God. There have been times in the supermarket when I've been so overwhelmed by the presence of God that I found myself leaning over the shopping cart; and people thought I was just trying to decide what can of pork 'n beans to buy that day. But I was really just thinking about the goodness of Jesus and all that He's done for me. And something just starts welling up on the inside of me that says, "You've got to praise Him!"

Maybe you think it's optional, but it's mandatory. You've got to praise Him! It was praising God that got you this far. It was praising God in the good times and in the bad times. It was praising Him when you felt like it and when you didn't. Don't let the rocks cry out! Give Him all the praise! When the praises go up, the blessings come down. Praise your God now and forevermore!

Think It Through

Explain what "the way UP is DOWN" means to you: _____
_____
_____

What is humility and why does God value it? _____
_____
_____

How does Jesus reveal Himself to you through your imperfections?
_____
_____
_____

How should you handle the praises of men? _____
_____
_____

Why is praising God so important? Give some examples from your life to illustrate this: _____
_____
_____

Day 13

Don't Be Deceived

"And do not be conformed to this world, but be transformed by the renewing of your mind, that you may prove what is that good and acceptable and perfect will of God."
~ Romans 12:2

Deception. There is so much of it going on in our world. Things have changed, and we must recognize that there is an intense opposition to truth as God defines it. There is a demonic agenda attempting to force its way on us and certainly intent on leading people, even the church, astray.

Just look at our media and entertainment. Things that used to grieve the people of God no longer grieve them. We see all kinds of ungodliness paraded before us and we wink at it. Immorality and profanity on TV and in the movies—not to mention all of the violence! "Well, it's just the way the world is." And that's precisely the problem: the things that grieve the Spirit of God no longer grieve us. It's as if we've been lulled to sleep. We need to come to grips with the fact that this blinding effect has found its way into the church. You heard me! The spirit of this age, seated in church pews, seeks to conform believers to the evils of the day, when believers should be making a difference. You and I should be making an impact that brings about transformation in our culture and our world.

Paul warned us not to be conformed to this world, but to be transformed by the renewing of our minds. (Romans 12:2). God's got a plan, a purpose in heaven that He wants fulfilled on earth. We should be praying and cooperating with Him that His will be done.

Why are we sitting back and letting the enemy have his way? Years ago we were horrified and grieved to hear that the courts legalized abortion. But how many times do we think about it now? It's just become a part of our culture. It's become a part of what we do. Well, they can legalize and legislate it, but *sin is still sin*. The problem is people want to redefine sin. People want to rewrite the Bible to eliminate any mention of sin. They're deceived into thinking "to each his or her own—it's my life and I'll do as I please!"

I came across a quote from evangelist Billy Graham that is so very powerful. He said, "Our society serves to avoid any possibility of offending anyone except God." Today we're consumed by political correctness at the expense of God's Word. Christians are so afraid of speaking out against sin and deception that it's got Satan dancing! These last days are tough... and they're only going to get tougher. Remember Paul told Timothy in 2 Timothy 4 that the time would come when people wouldn't be able to stand sound doctrine and teaching, but, instead would run around like a group of chickens frantically chasing this way and that, trying to find teachers who taught what they wanted to hear. And Paul warned that "they will turn their ears away from the truth and be turned aside to fables." That's deception, and we need to avoid it.

I want you to understand this, because, as a believer faced with deception, you must be prepared to respond. What happens when you're on the job and people begin to talk about racism or issues of immorality or crime — what are you going to say? Here's a little something for you to think about: A cat doesn't bark. A dog doesn't meow. A dog barks; a cat meows. It's according to their nature, right? So sinners are going to act like sinners: liars will lie, cheaters will cheat, thieves will steal. When you are faced with all of that, how will you respond?

I'm going to share a personal story about what happened one day when I told a lie. Me, little Larry, lying! I know that's a shocker, isn't it? I got in trouble about something and I figured, "Let me lie my way out of this." So I kept a straight face and I lied. Everything in me was lying. And my mother said, "All right now. Well, I'm going to go in the room and I'm going to pray, and I'm going to ask God about it. And God's going to tell me if you're lying or not." Now I knew she was tight with God, so I cried out, "Mommy, don't do that, I'm lying! So you might as well do what you're going to do now, because I told a lie!" I knew my mother walked with God, so I was sure God was going to tell on me!

You know every April we're confronted with this same choice: Do I lie...or do I tell the truth? You know April...Tax time! Whether you like it or not, if you choose to lie on your taxes, then you're acting like a liar! Hey, don't shoot the messenger now! I'm just telling it like it is!

Since I was a child, I heard saints say, "We're in the world, but we're not of the world." And yet, you and I have to live among people. We see each other daily at work, at school, in the supermarket. What makes us different is that we have a divine call to be a light in the darkness, to be the salt of the earth. That means we have to keep ourselves from being deceived so we can help others avoid deception as well.

How do we avoid deception? By staying close to Jesus. By reading the Word of God and meditating on it daily. By prayer, and fasting, if necessary. It's not always going to be easy. There's always going to be challenges. Life is full of them. But you can live clear-headed in God's truth.

We all came out of sin and deception of one form or another. Paul explained this to the Corinthian church in I Corinthians 6, when he mentioned a long list of their former sins. But he said in verse 11, "And such were some of you." You, too, have sinned and fallen short of the glory.

But note that little word "were." That means that's who you used to be. That's who I used to be. But we're not those people anymore. We've been washed, cleansed, delivered, sanctified, and set apart unto God, amen? We've been justified. Now you and I can live in newness of life, free from deception. And that's something to shout about!

Think It Through

List some of the deceptions of the world that believers must be on guard against: _____
_____
_____

How should we deal with deception? _____
_____
_____

Describe a situation in which you were faced with deception, and tell how you handled it: _____
_____
_____

How can you, as a Christian, avoid being deceived? _____
_____
_____

Write the Scripture that gives you the most help in defeating deception:
_____
_____
_____

Day 14

Keep It Real

"Now thanks be to God who always leads us in triumph in Christ, and through us diffuses the fragrance of His knowledge in every place."
~ 2 Corinthians 2:14

There is a spirit of skepticism in the world. People are not sure we are who we say we are as Christians. And that's not *all* the world's fault. Sometimes we've presented an off-brand Christianity that is so contradictory to what God has established that they can't be blamed for their skepticism! Men and women today go so far with certain elements of the gospel and completely ignore other themes. For instance, surely we're called to prosper, but Jesus did not hang on Calvary to get you a Maserati!

The world is hungry to see what authentic Christianity looks like. People are watching us. They may not say a word, but they're observing how we conduct our lives. They're watching to see if we say one thing and do another. They know there is power in God, but their minds are not often convinced of it when they look at His children. In a sense, you could say they are hoping to see authenticity in us!

The late Ray Steadman wrote a book I think every believer should read: *Authentic Christianity*. In it, he discussed five marks of the authentic

Christian. I'd like to share them with you, along with my thoughts.

Unquenchable Optimism. "Thanks be to God Who always leads us to triumph in Christ" (2 Corinthians 2:14). If anyone should be optimistic, it should be the people of God. But after pastoring a quarter of a century and in Christ longer than that, I've found that human nature is amazing. People can be good to a point and then retreat. They can have faith for a week, then go into doubt and unbelief. Where is the consistency? We should go through trying times and come out better than the Energizer Bunny! It's unfortunate when someone who doesn't know Jesus can be more optimistic than someone who knows Him. Make sure you're not one of the believers who is happy one day and sad the next. Our perspective should be different. What we go through here is a temporary experience. We must learn to take our eyes off what we see and look at what we can't see. It may not yet be real, but it *is* reality. This too shall pass!

Unvarying Success. Unvarying means always, consistently and without fail! There is never a time or a place when we are not triumphant in Christ Jesus. Never mind what it sounds, looks or feels like; we have been declared triumphant in Christ - always. Learn to declare it when the devil's breathing down your neck! You have the victory! You can say with confidence like the psalmist, "God is on *my* side" (Psalm 56:9). Despite hardships, things invariably and inevitably will work out for our good. Even the things working against us will work for us, so we can complete God's objective for our lives.

Back in 2 Corinthians 2:14, we read that God always leads us to triumph. This actually means He causes us to dance in victory. It's amazing to me how some people danced for the world and gave all their energy to the devil. Now that they're saved and sanctified, they stand still in church! Israel danced when they looked over their shoulders and saw the Red Sea close over their enemies. When was the last time you looked over your shoulder and saw how far He's brought you?

Unforgettable Impact. Note, it's through us that He "diffuses the fragrance of His knowledge in every place" (2 Corinthians 2:14). Authentic Christianity leaves an impression on all who encounter it. Because people are looking for real Christians, when they enter the room, they should sense a change in the atmosphere. The spirit of life should bring a fresh fragrance to the place!

Unimpeachable Integrity. God expects us to be men and women of integrity. That integrity is to be displayed in sincerity and honesty. It should be observed in our purpose originating from God. It should be seen in the sight of God, transparent to all investigation. And it should be found in Christ, in that all that we have and are is from Him. There's too much hypocrisy in the body today. The Word tells us that we're servants. I am a servant. You are a servant. Walk humbly! Walk in integrity. Speak the truth in love. Stop lying to one another! My mother always told us that liars have a place in the lake of fire (Revelation 21:8). You're a child of God; behave like your Father!

Undeniable Reality. (2 Corinthians 3:1-3) There has been a transformation in you, and you are having an impact on others. Whenever I get discouraged and think nothing in my life is working as I expected it to, I'm always reminded of someone I've poured into that shows a worthwhile change. That's the mark of an authentic Christian. You create change. Your words make a difference. If it doesn't seem like it yet, press on. You will see transformation in the lives of those you minister to. Just keep at it. Keep planting and watering seeds, knowing God is the God of increase and He will bring the harvest to pass!

Satan looks for those who are up to something good. He knows if he leaves you alone, you'll mess up his plans big time. This is why he sends distractions and hindrances against you. But you need to keep your eyes on Jesus. Keep focused! He wouldn't be fighting you this hard if you didn't have something great to offer. Wherever you are—in the world of education, the world of medicine, or the world of business—make a difference!

Think It Through

How is optimism evident in your daily walk with Jesus? _____
_____
_____

List ways in which difficulties can be opportunities for success: _____
_____
_____

In what ways can you make a positive impact on unbelievers? _____
_____
_____

How do you demonstrate integrity in your life?_____
_____
_____

Have you created change in someone's life? Briefly share how:_____
_____
_____

Day 15

It's Not Gonna Happen

"If God is for us, who can stand against us?" ~ Romans 8:31

Are you going through some challenges? Are you asking why you're being attacked, why the storm, why the difficulty? Beloved, anointed people always attract attention. That attention may be good or it may be bad. But I want you to remember that if you are in the midst of trouble, before you even get to the battlefield, the battle has already been won. This fight is fixed! You can go in knowing that things have been arranged for your victory. You can be at ease.

There may be parts of your situation that cause worry or terrorize you. We can't see the end from the beginning, but God can! He's still seated on the throne. The things that make you afraid, God laughs at. He sees the outcome we cannot even imagine.

David was fearful at times, too. He admitted it in Psalm 56. When we focus our attention on our circumstances instead of on God, fear always begins to knock at the door. But when fear knocks, you don't have to answer it! Starve your fear; feed your faith. One of the ways you do this is by trusting in God. You may not be able to keep fear from coming at you, but you can certainly prevent it from becoming a part of you. Keep your faith high. Trust in God and make a declaration that you will not be afraid, that you will trust regardless of the illusions you see around you.

In Psalm 56:9, David declares, "This I know, because God is for me." God is for you. Praise Him, because you wouldn't want Him against you! You know the Bible says that "if God is for us, who can stand against us?" (Romans 8:31). Remind yourself: *He's for me.*

God deserves our best praise. He turns what was meant for evil, toward us, into good. Unfortunately, we're often selective with the praise. As long as the conditions are right or things are going according to plan, we'll praise. Anyone can, under those circumstances! But can you praise God when all hell is breaking loose? Do you have to be prompted and persuaded to praise God for what He's done? I hope not! Praise is fitting for us to give, so don't let anything stop your praise.

Things may not be turning out—or have not turned out—as you desired, but each one of us has a testimony of fact and truth showing what God has done for us. From time to time, pause, look back and recall from where God has brought you. He's brought you a mighty long way. I want to encourage you: you've got history with God, and He's got a reputation that cannot be tainted.

You know, sometimes we hear, but we don't really grasp this as truth: "No weapon formed against you shall prosper, and every tongue that shall rise up against you in judgment, you shall condemn. This is the heritage of the servants of the Lord, and their righteousness is from Me" (Isaiah 54:17). God did not say weapons won't be formed. Just don't be scared: they're not going to work! Every weapon is defeated in Jesus' name.

Sometimes we get in this spot where we think God is concerned about everybody but us. People are looking into our crisis and assuming there must be sin involved. Not always! Enemy attack is consistent with our placement, position, anointing, gifting and calling. Sometimes you experience trouble simply because you're walking in righteousness! In fact, often, your trouble is a signal that you're in the will of God! In Numbers 22-23, we read that the King of Moab was threatened by Israel's presence. Likewise, you are more of a threat to the enemy than you realize.

Maybe you're thinking, "Why is my answer to prayer for everyone else, but not me?" You really want to rejoice with those who rejoice, but you wonder if God has forgotten about you. Shut that whisper of the enemy down! You *are* blessed. Get used to it. You haven't seen anything yet. He's about to bless you in epic proportions! If God promised it, He will do it. No one can reverse what He designs.

My friend, open your eyes with expectancy. See that there will be manifestation of everything God has promised. Has He given you promises? Maybe ten years ago? One year ago? Last week? Praise Him for every guarantee. Praise Him for making good on His word. Praise Him that you are blessed and highly favored of God.

One Sunday while teaching I said, "God is in trouble." The people were quiet and seemingly confused. Then I explained, "God is a very present help *in* trouble" (Psalm 46:1). You are not alone in your suffering, in your dilemma. He's there with you. I think about when Elisha contended with the King of Syria. The king sent his army after the prophet with fury. Elisha and his servant looked up at the approaching army of Syrians, but Elisha stayed calm, cool and collected. I can't help but imagine that his servant thought he was crazy! Elisha said calmly, "There are more with us than against." The servant knew how to count. There were countless soldiers and just two of them. But Elisha prayed for his eyes to be open, and when they were, the servant saw God's angelic hosts all around. From this day, believe you are that way! Things that used to worry you, overwhelm you, and send your blood pressure soaring, won't have that effect any more. It doesn't matter how many enemies have come around you; God has you surrounded.

You must remember that God is not a respecter of persons. If He did it for Shadrach, He'll do it for you. If He did it for Daniel, He'll do it for you. If God did it before, He can do it again. Encourage yourself with that. Be like David when he saw Ziklag on fire. When you can't find an encouraging word in the mouth of your peers, get alone with God. Encourage yourself in His faithfulness and then consult with Him: "What am I to do?" I believe that, like David, He'll give you the promise, "You shall pursue them and you shall recover all."

You can make it. What the enemy meant for evil is not going to happen. God will turn it around for good and make it work for your benefit.

Think It Through

How did David react when difficulties came his way? _____
_____
_____

When things get tough, how do you encourage yourself in the Lord?
_____
_____
_____

"No weapon formed against you shall prosper": What do these words mean to you? _____
_____
_____

List ways you can open your eyes with expectancy that God's promises will manifest in your life: _____
_____
_____

Share how God turned a bad situation into something good for you:
_____
_____
_____

Day 16

Desperate People Dig Ditches

"Make this valley full of ditches. For thus says the Lord, 'You shall not see wind, nor shall you see rain; yet this valley shall be filled with water.'"
~ 2 Kings 3:16

There's an old familiar saying, "Desperate times call for desperate measures." When you are truly in need, you will do whatever it takes to meet that need.

In 2 Kings 3, we read that the kings of Israel and Judah had gone to war against the Moabites. They had developed a military strategy that seemed like a good one, except that their line of supplies could not be sustained. They ran out of water. After wandering in the desert for seven days, they found themselves desperate and in a rut. A rut is a fixed routine or pattern that has become dull and unproductive, but it's hard to change.

Have you ever been in a critical place and you just didn't know what to do?

Desperation can be a good thing! The kings came to Elisha because they were desperate. They needed a quick solution to a very serious problem, but instead they received instructions. Elisha told them, "Make this valley full of ditches. For thus says the Lord, 'You shall not see wind, nor shall you see rain; yet this valley shall be filled with water.'"

I once heard Dr. Ernestine Cleveland Reems say something I've never forgotten: "Too many people think the blessings of God come on a gravy train with biscuit wheels. God will give you some things you have to fight for. Miracles are not magic tricks. Faith is not a lottery ticket. Faith is, in fact, a work order. Hope is confident expectation of the goodness of God."

You see, faith is preparing for something you cannot perceive. Some people want to see it before they believe it. Some people even say, "seeing is believing." That's how it goes in the world, but the kingdom principle is, "believing is seeing." Faith without works is dead, according to James 2:26. It's not good to simply say, "I believe;" you need to do what you believe. That's where the blessing is really found–in the doing (James 1:25). Faith is an action word.

Are you willing to cooperate with God? Are you willing to do your part?

Some people want God to wave a magic wand over them and make everything right. They would rather ask the preacher to pray that they shed twenty-five pounds on the spot rather than change their eating habits and begin working out. But some things only come by your engagement. Do you have what it takes? Sometimes you'll have to get up off the seat of "do-nothing" and be actively engaged with God.

Digging ditches sounds absurd. The command was to fill a desert valley with ditches, plural. Sometimes when you need a ridiculous blessing, you have to do some ridiculous things! The principle here is this: dig as deep and as much as you want to receive. Don't be like others who say they want to receive from God, but they'll only go as far as to dig one ditch. If you want great blessings, many blessings, dig many ditches!

Digging ditches is hard work! It's not the kind of job everyone wants.

Some think they're too smart to dig ditches. They think they're too cute or better than that. I know I'm not above digging ditches!

Digging ditches is preparation. People who won't praise, pray or give are not preparing for anything good. You reap what you sow. If you sow sparingly, you'll reap the same. If you go above and beyond in generosity, you can expect that kind of harvest.

At the word of the Lord, everyone in that valley began digging ditches, and they dug ditches all night long, preparing for the promise of water. In the morning, they paused and offered a grain offering to God. A grain offering is a gift given to God as an act of thanksgiving and praise for His blessings. You need to get this: after toiling all night long, digging ditches with just a word that there shall be water, they paused and gave God thanks and praise! Remembering what God has done, how He has blessed, is fuel for the soul.

Thanksgiving and praise also have a prophetic dimension. They look with eyes of faith into the future. They don't just concentrate on what God has already done and what He's doing right now; they look with great expectation internally, knowing that God is turning situations around. Dig those ditches! Praise the Lord like never before! Give like you've never given before! Serve like you've never served before!

The grain offering was made of fine flour, which pointed to Jesus, the Bread of Life. It was prepared with oil, symbolizing the Holy Spirit and His anointing. In this hour like never before, you need to give God anointed praise, because that will remove burdens and destroy yokes. You can't simply do what you're comfortable doing. You're going to have to get out of your comfort zone.

You might be saying, "You don't know how hard it is." These soldiers were exhausted from the desert sun. Their lips were parched. Still, they opened their mouths and blessed the Lord. If you're right there with them, you're in the perfect place! If you'll just follow the instructions of God, He'll come in and fill your valley with water. The prophet told them water would fill the valley. They didn't see a cloud or smell rain. You can't let your conditions dictate your praise. Everything may not seem right, but you have to make it right anyhow. Bless the Lord at all times!

Notice where they had to dig the ditches: not on the mountaintop, but in the valley. You know the valley is symbolic of your low times, your depressions. That's when the devil wants you to throw in the towel.

Notice something else: they dug ditches and gave a grain offering not just among friends, but in the presence of their enemies. The Moabites were checking them out while they were praising God. Friend, whenever we get in that place where we stop letting our struggles, challenges and issues dictate our praise, it doesn't matter who's looking, you'll invite God into your situation to turn things around!

The Bible says, "In the morning after they gave the grain offering, suddenly..." Expect "suddenlies," my friend. Sudden blessings, immediate breakthroughs! It was a flash flood that filled the valley with water! You can always depend on God to make good His word!

Some people won't praise God until they can see it, feel it, hear it, smell it. They cannot trust God based upon a word. It's not your job to figure out how God's going to do it. It's simply your job to cooperate with Him. That's your responsibility! Leave the details to God. Stop staying up all night trying to figure out how He's going to work this out. Trust me: you need some sleep! Rest your head on your pillow knowing God has your back and He has everything under control.

Dig as deep and as much as you want to receive. Don't patty-cake the Lord. Don't be prim and proper. Don't worry about who's looking. Do what you can do. You need to dig for your family, for your marriage, for your health, for your wealth. Praise Him!

Think It Through

How can desperation be a good thing? _____
_____
_____

Explain the difference between "seeing is believing" and "believing is seeing." _____
_____
_____

In what way(s) do you dig ditches for your blessings? _____
_____
_____

After digging ditches all night long, what did the Israelites do first thing in the morning? _____
_____
_____

What "suddenlies" have you experienced in your walk with God? _____
_____
_____

Day 17
Stay on Course

"Blessed (happy, fortunate, to be envied) are the undefiled (the upright, truly sincere, and blameless) who walk in the way [of the revealed will of God], who walk (order their conduct and conversation) in the law of the Lord (the whole of God's revealed will)." ~Psalm 119:1

Do you know what could happen if you don't stay on course in your Christian walk? Lives could be lost—and yours could be one of them! When you follow the intended path, you grow in maturity and obedience to God's will, and you tap into Jesus' power and authority. You become a conduit of eternal change, advancing the cause of Christ until your triumphant end!

The enemy knows this about you. He knows you're a threat, and so he plans distractions at every turn. His agenda is to create confusion, delay and discouragement so you'll become lax or lazy, producing mediocre results. Nothing would be more rewarding to him than for you to quit the race altogether, presuming that God is not faithful to fulfill His word to you.

There are many scriptures that remind us of the importance of dedication and perseverance. 2 Peter 1:10-15 encourages us to be even more diligent to make our call and election sure. In other words, make certain you carry out the effect of God's calling and selection of you every day of your life. Be conscious, aware and deliberate in what God has called you to do, in what He's anointed or gifted you to do.

Most likely, we'll run into opposition when staying on course. The Bible teaches us that we're *in* the world, but not *of* it. Jesus' words ring true in John 15:18-20, "If the world hates you, you know it hated Me before it hated you. If you were of the world, the world would love its own. Yet because you are not of the world, but I chose you out of it, therefore the world hates you." And while He may not prevent all opposition or take us out of this world, He *will* keep us in the midst of it (John 17:14-15).

As Christians, the Apostle Paul instructs us, "by the mercies of God, that you present your bodies a living sacrifice, holy, acceptable to God, which is your reasonable service. And do not be conformed to this world, but be transformed by the renewing of your mind, that you may prove what is that good and acceptable and perfect will of God" (Romans 12:1-2). We must be aware of the manner of our presentation daily. We must recognize that our worship isn't something we do, but what we are! You are a praise to God–*live that way!*

The world may have a certain mode of operation, but we're not of that world; we're of the kingdom of God. Things operate differently here. We are to do good to all –especially to those in the household of faith (Galatians 6:10). As believers, we are all part of the same family. We're a brotherhood of saints and our citizenship is in heaven (Philippians 3:20; Ephesians 2:19-22). Beyond that, we're not just part of the same family; we're part of the very same body (1 Corinthians 12:27)! You are part of the Body of Christ. Christ is anointed, and you are in Christ and Christ is in you, the Hope of Glory. Thus, *you* are anointed! You are designed to be successful in ministry and life!

To stay on course is to conduct yourself as is expected in the house of

God. It's time to stop living like the world and start living like the bride of Christ, set apart, sanctified and holy. God desires to position you for the days to come as light in darkness, that others may see your good works and glorify Him. He sets before you the choices of life and death, blessing and cursing. Choose life! The decisions you make today don't just impact you; they impact those with whom you associate. They affect your children and future children (Deuteronomy 30:19).

I'm reminded of the reprimand Elijah gave the Israelites at Mount Carmel. He said, "How long will you falter between two opinions? If the Lord is God, follow Him; but if Baal, follow him" (1 Kings 18:21). To falter is to halt, limp or waver. You can't go on straddling the fence forever. If you're found on that day still straddling, Jesus will say He never knew you.

I am constantly perplexed that men and women who have witnessed the saving power of God can fall back into old, worldly practices, sin and rebellion. How is that? Did they forget the bondage and slavery?!

Beloved, stay on course. There's a blessing when you stay on course. There's deliverance and healing when you stay on course. And you must only do four things to remain:

Be decisively and insistently committed. Be real. Joshua said, "As for me and my house, we will serve the Lord" (Joshua 24:15). Make up your mind and remain firm on it. Mothers and fathers, get back to the job of parenting. Your children don't pay you rent. Set boundaries. Ensure they know how a godly home operates.

Earnestly contend for the faith. Jude 3-4 warns us that certain men have crept in unnoticed, turning the grace of God into lewdness and denying Him and Jesus Christ. There's conflict; the enemy is actively trying to steal your faith. Be earnest in battle.

Let no man deceive you. In Matthew 24:4-8, Jesus tells us the signs of the age, that many will come to deceive others. Don't miss the signs; don't allow anyone to rob you of truth, sanity or spirituality.

Love sincerely and completely. Jesus goes on in verse 12 of Matthew 24 to say that the love of many will wax cold. We are to put on love, the bond of perfection, and abound in love to all (Colossians 3:14; 1 Thessalonians 3:12-13). In this way, our hearts will be established as blameless in holiness before God.

One day, I want to hear God say, "Good and faithful servant, well done." Don't you? We're not promised tomorrow to get it together. Some will die in their 40s. Some younger than that. How will you stand in His presence?

Let's make the commitment that we will serve the Lord. Let's submit to what God has for us, because when we do, we'll experience the blessing that comes to those who are undefiled in the way. The blessing is in the doing. You'll become a magnet that attracts those blessings.

Think It Through

What are some of the benefits of staying on course with God? _____
_____
_____

Why do you run into opposition as you endeavor to stay on course?
_____
_____
_____

Of the four points listed (for staying on course) which, if any, do you struggle with? _____
_____
_____

What can you do to overcome that struggle (or those struggles)? _____
_____
_____
_____

What happens when you submit to what God has for you? _____
_____
_____

Day 18

Get Behind Me, Satan

"And Jesus answered and said to them: 'Take heed that no one deceives you.'"
~ Matthew 24:4

There is a severe spiritual ADD in the land—that's right, a spiritual deficit disorder. Many individuals can only hone in on the things of God for 2-3 minutes at a time before their attention is diverted! They succumb to an unfocused spirit, allowing the ploys of the enemy to be successful in keeping them from what is most important: the things of God. Considering the times, this should be far more alarming and troubling than we make it to be.

In Matthew 24, Jesus warned His disciples that deception would be on the rise in the end times. He said, "Take heed that no one deceives you." To be deceived is to be misled by false appearance or statement, to be deluded. Look around: this type of deception runs rampant today!

Why does an enemy with so many tactics use deception so widely? Because it works! Unsuspecting people are easy to deceive. We, as the body of Christ, need to wake up to the subtle lies. We need to rebuke the devil and remind him he's a defeated foe.

In 2 Corinthians 11:3, we see the Apostle Paul's concern that just as the serpent deceived Eve, the Christian mind could be corrupted from the simplicity of Christianity. He told Timothy that in the latter times, "some would leave the faith, giving heed to deceiving spirits and the doctrines of demons, having their own conscience seared as with a hot iron" (1 Timothy 4:1-2). It's unfortunate that many have and will leave the faith only to discover in the end they've been tricked. This is one of the greatest tragedies; the deceived are the last to realize they've been deceived!

I'm reminding you today to open your eyes. You determine if the enemy is successful in deceiving you. All things start as a seed and develop into a harvest. Be on the lookout! Guard your heart and mind in Christ Jesus.

Maybe you think you've got it under control, that this warning applies to everyone but you. I'd like you to remember the Apostle Peter. One day, Jesus asked His disciples, "Who do men say that I am?" Peter declared, "You are the Christ, Son of the Living God!" This was a revelation from the Spirit of God to Peter. He knew who Jesus was, and Jesus called Peter blessed because of it.

Shortly thereafter, just that quick, he was deceived. Jesus was once again talking to His disciples, sharing that He would die and rise on the third day. Peter rebuked Jesus, saying, "Far be it from You, Lord; this shall not happen to You!" (Matthew 16:21-23). The information Jesus was giving His disciples was vital. Peter's comment demanded an instant response. Thus, without hesitation Jesus turned to Peter (He got in his face) and said, "Get behind me, Satan. You are an offense to Me, for you are not mindful of the things of God."

Here we see what *not to do* in Peter's distraction and what *to do* in Jesus' reaction!

Protect your heart and mind. There is a blessing that comes with revelation. Hosea 4:6 warns us that people are destroyed for the lack of it. It isn't that revelation is ever unavailable, but that men and women reject what is made available. Determine not to toss aside what God has revealed or to minimize it. Instead, embrace it and allow its entrance to bring light to your understanding (Psalm 119:130). Revelation discloses and exposes truth. It expels darkness. It showcases the will of God and His desire for His people. It orders our steps *and* our stops.

Resist the devil and he will flee. When the enemy wants to introduce something contrary to the will of God, don't entertain or play with him. Speak up and say, "Get behind me, Satan." This expression means, "Get out of my way." Refuse to allow the enemy's tactics to be an offense or stumbling block to God's will for your life. Don't be deceived and destroy your life.

3. **Praise God and live right.** The Bible tells us that whoever praises God glorifies Him, and "to him who orders his conduct aright, I will show the salvation of God" (Psalm 50:23). You will be rescued from distraction as you focus on praising your Savior. Not only will you be rescued, but you will experience increase. Psalm 37:4 says, "Delight yourself in the Lord, and He will give you the desires of your heart." Delight is not just an occasional activity; it's a lifestyle of worship. As you bring Him glory by your walk, He will bestow on you the very desires that pulse within your heart. He will bring you increase, revelation, wisdom, insight, understanding–"great and mighty things"–as you call upon Him (Jeremiah 33:3).

The enemy wants you off track. He's telling you to go left when God says to go right. He's telling you to withhold when God's saying to give. He's telling you to be bitter when God is saying to forgive. Don't give him one moment of time. Look him in the face and say, "Get out of my way." When you resist him, he will flee.

Be aware: your enemy might not come looking like an enemy. He might come looking like a member of the church of God. But if he (or she) is promoting something that leads others astray, you need to declare, "Get behind me. Hate me if you must; I have a job to do and a journey to finish. I will not be distracted from it!" Determine not to be derailed. Remind yourself who Jesus is. Get a revelation and hold fast to it.

Don't forget that the same Peter who announced, "You are the Christ," and then got distracted by the enemy was also given the keys to the kingdom. Jesus said to him in Matthew 16:19, "Whatever you bind on earth will be bound in heaven, and whatever you loose on earth will be loosed in heaven." These keys were given to us all, and they denote privilege, access and authority in God's kingdom. Today, there are some doors out there that need to be opened, doors that no man can shut. He's given you access, but you have to use it. Though the enemy will try his best to intimidate us from our authority, all we need to do is exercise our rights to put him in his place. Loose grace! Loose deliverance! You've come this far in Christ Jesus. Keep moving forward. Tell the enemy to get behind!

Let's pray: Father, grant me revelation, determination and resolve, that I will not succumb to the powers that be, but stand focused and discerning. Help me to resist the enemy and stay the course until I receive the price. Forgive me for times when I've been distracted and entrapped, and help me to fulfill the great destiny You have prepared for me. It's all for Your glory. Amen.

Think It Through

Why is it so hard for many Christians to focus on the things of God?
_____
_____
_____

What is one of the major tools of the enemy, and why does he use it so much? _____
_____
_____

"You determine if the enemy is successful in deceiving you." Explain what this means and why it is so important: _____
_____
_____

Why is it difficult sometimes to discern the enemy in our midst? _____
_____
_____

List the three points that will help you to discern and overcome the deceptive tactics of the enemy: _____
_____
_____

Day 19

Be Angry and Sin Not

"Be angry and sin not." ~ Ephesians 4:26

Did you know that anger is a God-given emotional response? Did you know it's not only normal but okay for you to get angry?

Dr. Gary Chapman, in his book, *Anger: Taming a Powerful Emotion,* says, "Anger is really a cluster of emotions, involving the body, mind, and will and is a response to some event or situation in life that causes us irritation, frustration, pain or other displeasure. Anger is fed by feelings of disappointment, hurt, rejection and embarrassment." When things are not as we think they should be, we experience anger—even if it's over something relatively minor, like being cut off in rush hour traffic.

Too often, as Christians, we feel that anger is wrong. We should never be angry. But I want you to consider the text in Ephesians 4:26: It says, "Be angry and sin not." Anger can be legitimate. It is not good or bad in and of itself. It's our response to the anger that makes it sinful or not. So, as long as we're managing it correctly, it is fine. It's only when we lose control that anger becomes a bad thing.

Anger, when controlled, can help us solve life's problems. We see Jesus' anger expressed when He found the money-changers in the temple (Matthew 21:12). He didn't wag His finger and say, "Don't you do that!" The Bible says He was angry: He overturned the money-lenders' tables and started whipping them. That was righteous indignation: anger focused in the right way. You see it's not that you *cannot* be angry. A good brother in the Lord once told me, "If anyone makes you feel like you can't be angry legitimately, that's manipulation, that's control—and you should reject it."

However, not every display of anger is good. Anger can be like leaping into an incredibly responsive sports car, gunning the engine and taking off at a high speed…only to discover that the brakes are out of order. Benjamin Franklin said, "Whatever is begun in anger ends in shame." Eleanor Roosevelt said, "Anger is one letter short of danger." This is because we usually release anger in one of two ways: *exploding or imploding*. Explosive anger comes in the form of yelling or some violent action. Implosive anger shows itself as passive aggression, huffing and puffing, or talking under one's breath.

Sometimes we feel anger because we feel vulnerable or powerless. We may feel afraid. Other times, we feel anger because our goal or purpose is blocked. We may have suppressed something painful until, like a ball submerged in water, our anger pops to the surface.

Dr. Robert Fraum said that we can know we have a problem with anger if our anger is too intense or powerful, or if it lasts a long time and occurs frequently. These are signs of an anger disorder or an anger management problem. Now, angry feelings or aggressive behavior do not necessarily indicate a problem with anger. Just because you blew it one time does not mean you have an anger problem. But there is a line: It's a respect line. If you cross that line in your anger, there are repercussions.

Unhealthy anger is the opposite of love. Whereas love draws you toward a person, anger sets you against the one who sparked the anger. Dr. Redford Williams, professor of psychology at Duke University Medical

Center, wrote a book called *In Control*, which gives seven signs that you or someone you love may be on anger overload:

Getting mad over little things: People who get upset about trivial things, like being cut off by another driver or having to wait for Canadian Geese to cross the road are likely to have an anger problem.
Getting red in the face: Your body is affected by what is going on inside of you. You get mad over little things, and your face shows it!
Interrupting: Angry people tend to be impatient people. You have trouble waiting for people to finish what they are saying. You have to jump in and express yourself on serious matters.
Being a complainer. Nothing is good enough for you. There's always something negative to remark.
Being overly sensitive: People feel as if they have to walk around on eggshells with you. This is especially frustrating if it's in their own house.
Being cold-hearted: You hear of terrorist attacks or community tragedies and you shrug it off like, "Well, that's just how it is."
Holding a grudge: You have difficulty forgiving someone who wronged you in the past. Being wronged is often the case in human relationships, whether with family, friends, or co-workers. If you like to hold grudges, think about this: How would you like God to hold grudges against you? Let it go!

If you have trouble coping with anger or controlling rage, I want to encourage you to confess the problem. The Bible tells us in 1 John 1:9 that if we confess our sins, He is faithful and just to forgive our sins and cleanse us from all unrighteousness. Don't repress your anger. Don't stuff it down inside you or pretend it didn't happen. If you do, you'll just explode at a later date and cause even more damage to yourself and to those around you. Conversely, don't express your anger the wrong way. There is a right way to express this emotion. If you take time to breathe and think, you'll be less likely to hurt yourself or others and then have to make amends. Finally, remember that the greatest tool you have to help you handle anger is prayer. When you ask the Lord, He will help you deal with it.

Often, anger is nothing more than a cover for frustration, fear or hurt. Identify the root or source of that emotion. Who is the real culprit? You're yelling at your wife, but could it be that you're mad at your mother? You're yelling at your husband, but could it be that you're really angry with your employer? You're yelling at your son when it could be you're upset with his daddy.

Identify your unfulfilled need. Remember: anger, fear, hurt, frustration—there's a need not being met there. Figure out an alternative constructive action. Punching the wall does no real good. Come up with a different approach. Take specific action. Once you've identified your constructive alternative, act on it. Claim your right to resolve the source of your anger and reclaim your life. And seek help. Asking for help doesn't make you weak. It suggests strength.

In closing, consider the advice of Dr. Phil MacGraw. When feeling angry, he says: "Reframe: Ask yourself what really matters. If you are in touch with your authentic self, you really are what matters most. Relax, take a deep breath: if you're angry count to ten; if you're really angry, count to one hundred. Maybe you just need to take a walk. React rationally: Stop thinking the world revolves around you! When you have a false sense of urgency or an inflated sense of self-importance, you set yourself up for failure."

It has been said that for every minute you are angry, you lose sixty seconds of happiness. Be angry...sin not. Don't let the sun go down on your wrath. Treat it with urgency. Don't let the enemy consume you with anger, wrath or rage. God wants us to use our anger and righteous indignation to make things right in this world. Let's do it for the glory of God!

Think It Through

What is anger? _____
_____
_____

Is it always wrong to be angry? _____
_____
_____

List some of the reasons you feel anger: _____
_____
_____

Which, if any, of the seven signs of anger overload do you struggle with?
_____
_____
_____

What can you do to overcome these anger problems? _____
_____
_____

Day 20

God Always Has a Strategy

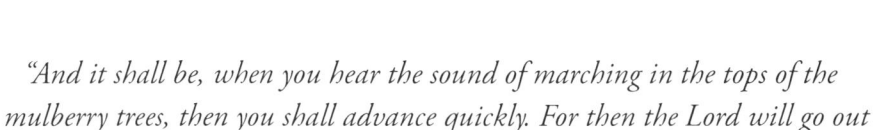

"And it shall be, when you hear the sound of marching in the tops of the mulberry trees, then you shall advance quickly. For then the Lord will go out before you to strike the camp of the Philistines." ~ 2 Samuel 5: 24

The word is out concerning you, my friend. You are anointed! Your anointing is powerful, conspicuous, attractive. It's not mystical, but the manifest presence and power of God that is particularly evident in and upon your life as a believer.

As far as the anointing is concerned, you either have it or you don't. Until David was anointed king over Israel, he had no personal enemies. Once he was anointed, they began to plan attacks against him (2 Samuel 5:17-25)! David discovered not only his calling, but also his enemies.

The Philistines spread themselves across the Valley of Rephaim, which means, "the valley of giants." We all will face giants at some point. Giants are anything that distract our focus from God, deter us from our service to God, and drain us of our driving passion for God. There are many giants. You may have met those of fear, anxiety, worry, loneliness, guilt, shame, pride, jealousy, selfishness, lust and greed already on your journey. Giants can be intimidating, but there's no need for you to be afraid or bow. If God allows a giant in your life, He allows it with purpose. That may be to test your faith so you can experience victory. No trials, no triumphs. You can't have a testimony without a test!

O. S. Hawkins said, "A problem is the platform upon which God desires to show how wonderful He can provide." Our God has never performed a miracle that did not begin at the platform of a problem. If you have a problem, you're in the right place for God to show up and show out on your behalf!

David, upon hearing that his enemies had come out in full force against him, inquired of the Lord. Please note that. In critical times, be sure to get a word from the Lord! Don't ever become presumptuous in your anointed self. David didn't assume to act; he prayed about it. Prayer requires humility.

God gave David a strategy that day that delivered the Philistines into his hands. He named the spot of their defeat *Baal Perazim*, or "Lord of the Breakthrough." My friend, your breakthrough is in the strategy. God always has a strategy.

Isn't it amazing that as you're celebrating victory over one thing, here comes something else to test your faith? While David was still rejoicing over his victory in the valley, the Bible says the Philistines came out in full force once more against him. Don't think you're just going to have one attack in your anointed life. The attacks will be relentless. The good news is that your victory is also relentless!

Bishop T.D. Jakes correctly contends, "For every struggle in your life, there is a strategy." God has a strategy for your family, your habit, your money, your attitude–for everything! Sometimes, however, those strategies sound ridiculous. Consider Moses in front of the Red Sea, and God said, "Stretch out your hand." Or Joshua outside the fortified walls of Jericho, who was told to march around the wall for six days, and on the seventh day of marching, the wall would fall down. How about Samson, who was inspired to use the jawbone of a dead donkey to defend himself? Then there was Jesus who told the disciples to feed 5,000+ men with five small fish and two loaves of bread. There is always a strategy from God, but it often will sound crazy. If you submit to it, though, it will work!

Here, the Philistines had spread themselves once again across the Valley of Giants, and we see David inquire of the Lord a second time (verse 23). This was true humility, because David could have simply gone off the word given to him by God previously. He could have assumed he knew how to handle his own affairs. Instead, he inquired of the Lord a second time! Please do not assume that God will always duplicate deliverance methods. God is not that predictable! Don't limit His methods. And don't get cocky. You're sure to fail if you think you've got this on your own.

God desires cooperation! He already knows everything about your enemy, the giant, the problem. Trust Him enough to submit to His purpose and plan. Don't allow your relationship with Him to grow stale. Keep it fresh every morning. I've discovered that whenever we truly minister to the Lord, as described in Acts 13, the Holy Spirit will speak. The problem we often have is that we give God no time, so we cannot hear Him speaking. We insist on doing things our own way, and we come up empty-handed every time. When will you pause for a moment, shut it down, and spend time with God until you hear from Him?

If God's ever done it before, He can do it again. He can bring you victory over your enemies. You just have to trust Him. Acknowledge Him with all your heart and lean not to your own understanding. This time, it's going to be big, just like it was last time, and God's name will be glorified through your trust in Him!

The anointing removes burdens and destroys yokes (Isaiah 10:27). Anything that's broken may likely be repaired, but when it's destroyed, that's it! It cannot be repaired. It cannot hold you captive or hold you back anymore! That's the anointing of the power of the living Christ at work within us!

When purpose and destiny converge, things can get a little turbulent. Your anointing will be celebrated by some, but it will be intimidating to others. It will cause some people to treat you like you are far more important than you could ever be. It will attract every kind of hater—even ones who don't know you! But keep in mind: the anointing of God is not about you; it's all about Jesus!

The touch of God will make a difference. The enemy knows the touch of God on you is dangerous, and that's why he wants to shut down what you're doing. He knows if he leaves you alone, anointed people will do what anointed people do: remove burdens, set captives free and frustrate his plans!

Like David, you have been anointed, graced of the Lord, fully resourced, selected and set apart. Yes, there are attacks and, yes, there are giants you must face. I pray you take seriously this word I've shared with you today and implement it immediately. I want you to see victory in every area of your life. My hope is that you will have such a hunger and thirst for God that you do not just inquire of Him often, but always! Never allow presumption to take the place of genuine faith in God. Doing so is foolishness. Doing so is dangerous. Do not be just a hearer of the Word, but a doer also. Only in Christ will you see giants die and find lasting victory today and in the days to come.

Think It Through

What are some of the "giants" we often face in life? _____
_____
_____

What "giants" have you faced, or are facing now? _____
_____
_____

Should you keep your focus on God? _____
_____
_____

"The power of the living Christ within us destroys yokes." What does this mean to you? _____
_____
_____

Why is the enemy afraid of the anointing on your life? _____
_____
_____

Day 21

Lead By Example

"You became followers of us and of the Lord, having received the word in much affliction, with joy of the Holy Spirit, so that you became examples to all." ~ 1 Thessalonians 1:6-7

In embarking upon any new season, our minds naturally assess what the past contained and what we hope will be different in the future. We often dwell on circumstances, the side effects, the details, rather than seeking out the root cause of our "problems" and determining to make changes there. This is why so many diets are begun and not finished, and resolutions are made only to be adjusted to something "more realistic" within the first 30 days.

I want to challenge you to consider a root, a foundation that, if adjusted, will lead you to a better end. I want to be a friendly reminder to you of how important it is to do what Jesus did. William J. Bennett said, "We—all of us, but especially the young—need around us those who possess a certain nobility, a largeness of soul and qualities of human experience worth imitating and striving for." I'm asking you to choose to imitate Christ. Will you make the resolution to deliberately lead by example?

You are a leader. This may come as a surprise to you. You might be thinking, "Not me," but you're only looking at earthly position and title. Having a leader's title is somewhat misleading. Many people say they're leaders, but have no followers; they are just taking a walk! They demand many things, but a true leader doesn't have to demand anything—certainly not respect. It comes with the territory! Yes, *you* are a leader, and you lead by example whether you intend to or not.

Leadership is essentially the process whereby an individual influences others to achieve a common goal. The critical word here is "influence." Leadership is influence. If you influenced your child to clean his or her room, then you are a leader, and an exceptional one at that.

You are influential. Jesus said in Matthew 5:13, "You are the salt of the earth." Salt not only seasons but preserves. If you live in the Northeast, you know it also melts ice. Likewise, we affect others by seasoning, flavoring, preserving and even melting hardened hearts. Jesus went on to say in verse 14, "You are the light of the world." We don't cast *our* light; we reflect the light of Jesus Christ. "Let your light so shine before men, that they may see your good works and glorify your Father in heaven." In other words, lead by example.

You are powerful. You're not some average Joe. You're so powerful that when you, with the light of Jesus, walk into a dark room, darkness must give way to you. Wherever you are, things have to change. You have that kind of power! Unfortunately, too many of us are living far below our privilege and power. We need to stir up the gift of God in us so that His glory can be seen in our lives.

When we tap into our power *in* Christ, we behave *like* Christ - this is what captures people's attention! Remember, Jesus said He did not come into the world to be served, but rather to serve. This is difficult for supposed leaders who are demanding and arrogant, who think the world revolves around them and that they should be catered to. They act powerful, but have no true power. Jesus came and He served. 1 Peter 2:21 says,

"Christ suffered for us, leaving us an example, that you should follow His steps."

Jesus Himself explained that His every action – His every choice, personal interaction and teaching moment – were purposed to teach us how to lead. He said, "I've given you an example, that you should do as I have done to you" (John 13:15). Don't try to reinvent the wheel; copy the Perfect Wheel and get moving!

Don't keep us waiting. Paul said in Romans 8:19 that creation eagerly awaits the revealing of the sons of God. Mankind needs to see the love of God, His mercy and grace. We need to see truth, character and integrity in the children of God. Don't keep us waiting.

Somebody's watching you. Show them who you are: "You are a chosen generation, a royal priesthood, a holy nation, God's own special people" (1 Peter 2:9). 24 hours a day, seven days a week, proclaim the praises of Him who brought you out of darkness into His marvelous light. That means you are to walk in love, mercy and humility and to do justly to all people in your workplace or community, the local mall or grocery store.

Somebody's watching you. Don't blow it. You're going to be tempted in one way or another, but that doesn't mean you have to fall. Peter warned us, "I beg you… abstain from fleshly lusts which war against the soul" (1 Peter 2:11). If there were no potential for you to fall victim, he wouldn't have told you to abstain. Be mindful that because you are a human being, sometimes you will be challenged—especially with people. People can be frustrating, manipulative and irritating. Smile, be nice, be gracious to people. Abstain from those fleshly lusts. You never know who's watching. You never know where they are in life, and you don't want them to miss their day of visitation. Give them a *good* show!

Somebody's watching you. You will have haters. They will talk, but don't let what they say about you be true! Consider Titus 2:7-8 (AMP): "Show your own self in all respects to be a pattern and a model of good deeds and works, teaching what is unadulterated, showing gravity [having the strictest regard for truth and purity of motive], with dignity and seriousness. And let your instruction be sound and fit and wise and wholesome, vigorous and irrefutable and above censure, so that the opponent may be put to shame, finding nothing discrediting or evil to say."

Lead by example. Be committed. Don't let the cares of this life choke you. Rather, walk in the way of the Lord. Trust Him. It's going to be inconvenient for you on many occasions to reject what *you* want in order to embrace what *He* wants. Don't be a hearer only; be a doer of the Word. Lead by example. People don't want to hear you preaching; they want to see this life you say you have in Christ lived out before their eyes. Lead and love without hypocrisy—that's the Word of God!

Today, all day and every day, be like Christ. Allow His light and His love to fill you and flow through you. As you do, you will attract the attention of those who need to hear the gospel. Then lead by your godly example, so others will come to know the life-changing power of that gospel.

Think It Through

What makes you a leader? _____
_____
_____

In what ways (according to Matthew 5:13) are you to be "influential"?
_____
_____
_____

Is real power demonstrated through serving, or being served? Explain your answer: _____
_____
_____

"Somebody's watching you." Does knowing this affect the way you act? How? _____
_____
_____

How can you lead by example? _____
_____
_____

SECTION THREE

FINISH STRONG

Day 22

It's Time to Break the Cycle

"And the Lord spoke to me, saying: "You have skirted this mountain long enough."" ~ Deuteronomy 2:2-3

For some, today is absolutely wonderful, filled with bountiful blessings and incredible opportunities. But for others, today is extremely hard, filled with persistent frustrations and constant disappointments. If you most identify with the latter, I believe my purpose is to tell you, "You've circled this mountain long enough. It's time to break the cycle!"

Deuteronomy 2:1-3 tells of a time when Moses and the children of Israel were on the East Bank of the Jordan, preparing to enter the Promised Land. It says, "Then we turned and set out for the wilderness by the way of the Red Sea, as the Lord spoke to me, and circled Mount Seir for many days. And the Lord spoke to me, saying, 'You have circled this mountain long enough. Now turn North...'" At the end of verse 3, God instructed the Israelites, "Now turn north." After having been enslaved for 430 years, they were about to go into the place that God had promised them, a land flowing with milk and honey (prosperity). Now remember: These were the new generation of Israelites—the previous generation had died in the wilderness. Yet here they were, circling Mount Seir, when God said, "You have circled this mountain long enough."

Life is filled with circles—cycles and seasons that we all go through. Sometimes they're easy; sometimes not. Sometimes it feels like you're on a merry-go-round, minus the "merry!" You just can't seem to get ahead. Every time you make a little progress, you're pulled right back into the circle, experiencing defeat and negative situations time and time again.

Sonny and Cher lived with the family when I was a child—no, not the singing duo—ours were gerbils. The little mouse-like mammals came with those names, so we kept them. They were in a cage, but rodents like gerbils and hamsters have to be on the move. So they had an exercise wheel—and they'd get on that wheel and run and run and run. They weren't getting anywhere; they were just moving about. Some of us are like that. We're on a wheel and we're moving, but we're not getting anywhere.

If you're feeling a little like Sonny or Cher, then you've got to break the cycle! The first step is to understand the reason(s) you find yourself in it. Here are a few reasons I've discovered:

Some people are stuck in time. They're marching around in the circle of their past memories, whether good or bad. Some people are just hanging out in yesterday and yesteryear. They're moving, but there's no momentum.

Some people are stuck in relationships. They can't seem to move ahead; there's no growth. They've settled for "fine," and I have heard that "fine is the enemy of fantastic."

Some people are stuck in health. They just can't seem to move forward into better health. Every time one symptom begins to clear up, other symptoms start to appear! Powerlessness and hopelessness can easily take root in situations like these.

Some people are stuck in money. They just got a huge raise six months ago, but for some reason, they *still* have more month than money. Often, they've raised their level of living without even being aware and the new fruit is swallowed up in unnecessary expenditures or paying off past debts.

Some people are stuck in joblessness. They're always blaming the situation on somebody—an unfair boss, discrimination, coworker sabotage—but it's not somebody, it's *them*. They can't get off the hamster wheel.

Israel experienced this wandering… forty years going around in circles! We can look at Israel and criticize them, but all of us at one time or another have committed the same sin. God has been good to us, God has blessed us; yet we seem to forget His goodness, and we go back to our old ways. Do you think that God delivered the Israelites from 430 years of bondage in Egypt just so they could wander in circles in the wilderness for forty years? Absolutely not! Egypt represents oppression and sin; Pharaoh represents Satan. Do you think God delivered you and me from sin and from Satan, so that we could just make circles for the rest of our lives, never fulfilling our purpose, never coming into peace and prosperity? Again, the answer is no! But many of us forfeit the blessings of God because we have our own agendas, our own ways, and we do just what Israel did.

Today, I promise you, if you don't make a change, it'll be a "new day" but it will be an "old you." And an "old you" in a "new day" will not be profitable. You've got to make some changes, friend, or else this year you'll be in the same predicament as you were last year. You've got to break the cycle!

I want to challenge you today to keep your eyes on the promise and not on the giants in the land. And if you will keep your eyes on the promise, you will go into the land, slay all the giants, and enjoy what the Lord has for you! Paul said it this way: "I don't consider myself as having apprehended, but one thing I do: forgetting those things which are behind and reaching toward those things that are ahead, I press on toward the mark of the prize for the high calling of God in Christ Jesus." Don't allow yourself to get stuck in circles. Like Paul, press on for the prize, no matter how tough the "going" may be.

Some people want the blessing, but they don't want to go through the process of attaining the blessing. However, the process is crucial to your faith-development. It is only through this process that you will go in and possess the land.

When all is said and done, *you* are responsible for where you are right now. Maybe you've been handed some hard knocks, some challenges in life, but you have a decision to make about how you will react or respond to things that come.

I'm going to share a truth with you: If you want something you've never had, you've got to do something you've never done. If you've been on this "hamster wheel" and things haven't worked out for you, you need to make a shift; you need to make a change. You have circled this mountain long enough. You have pitied yourself long enough. You have bickered long enough. You have rebelled against God long enough. You have talked about your brothers and sisters long enough. You have held back what is right long enough. *Time to break the cycle!*

You want to be blessed? Well, your blessing is in an elevated place and it's going to require some movement on your part to get there. God wants us to move higher, but some people refuse, because they've grown comfortable with what's down. If that's you today, come out of the mundane! God wants you to step into this place of purpose, to change your position and direction. He wants you to truly experience His blessings. God says, "I have something new I want to do in your life." The promise is now. Enter your promised land!

Think It Through

What is the first step in breaking any cycle of behavior? _____
_____
_____

Which of the five listed reasons for becoming stuck are problem areas for you? _____
_____
_____

List ways you can get off the "hamster wheel": _____
_____
_____

Why do the blessings of God often come through a process that involves struggle? _____
_____
_____

Why should you, as a believer, avoid complacency in your life? _____
_____
_____
_____

Day 23

I Can Do This!

"But prove yourselves doers of the word, and not merely hearers."
~ James 1:22

I can do this! Those are four little words, but they carry a lot of weight when you choose to do what is right in God's sight. For instance, Matthew 5:44 tells us to "love your enemies. Bless those who curse you, do good to those who hate you, pray for those who spitefully use you and persecute you." Those commands may seem hard, but 1 John 5:3 tells us, "His commandments are not burdensome." Let that sink in a moment: His commandments are not burdensome. In other words they are not irksome, oppressive or grievous!

God does not ask us to do hard things; He asks us to do impossible things—things that cannot be done outside of Jesus Christ. But whenever God asks us to do something that is impossible, He also anoints us to do it. He provides the will, the means, and the grace to do everything He commands us to do. His anointing will break through every obstacle we may encounter.

Wayne Stiles said this: "We won't experience the joy of God's power if we keep running from impossible situations." If God asks impossible things of us, He plans to do the impossible for us. God will lead you and guide you in such a way that transformation is the end result. God may allow you to go into a fiery furnace, but you will come out with a testimony, fireproof and triumphant!

What happens when we avoid hard things? The answer is, hard things come to us. Have you ever tried to escape something that was difficult only to run right into it? There's a class that you've got to take in the school of the Holy Spirit, and that is the class of Hard Knocks. But look in the mirror and tell yourself, *"I can do this!"*

Difficulties arise because we need to learn to confront life from a different perspective that comes with a new set of values. When we walk contrary to the way of the world, there will be difficulties. Our friends won't understand us. It's as if we're speaking a foreign language. We're talking holiness; they're talking ungodliness. We're talking righteousness; they're talking unrighteousness.

Difficulties also exist for our growth potential. God will stretch us: This can be painful at times, because it requires leaving our comfort zones.

Scripture is full of examples of people who didn't want to do what God told them to do. Moses struggled with God's command to confront Pharaoh about freeing the children of Israel. And Jonah didn't want to go to Nineveh, so he purchased a ticket to somewhere else. He ended up in the belly of a big fish until he repented. Then God delivered him, and he went on to Nineveh.

Jesus said, "Come to Me all you who labor and are heavy laden, and I will give you rest. Take My yoke upon you and learn of Me; for I am gentle and lowly in heart and you will find rest for your souls; for My yoke is easy and My burden is light" (Matthew 11:28-30). Note: "My yoke is easy"...*but it's still a yoke.* "My burden is light"...*but it's still a burden.* The good news is we don't have to carry it alone.

Here are five things you can do through Christ, when faced with difficulties:

Be determined to do God's will: When Jesus was in the garden of Gethsemane (Matthew 26:30-46), He struggled in regards to the bitter cup, wrestling with the purpose that the Father had set out before Him–so much so that blood, like drops of sweat, poured from Him. Yet He said, "Not My will but Your will be done!"

Obey the Lord, no matter how silly or difficult it may appear: In 2 Kings 5:1-14 we read about Naaman, a valiant man, a champion among his people. The Bible says Naaman was a leper. He was also a proud man. He had heard about a prophet in Israel and decided to go to him for a healing. So he left with his entourage to see Elisha and when he arrived at the place where the prophet resided, Elisha didn't even come out to greet him. Instead, he sent his servant who told him, "Go down and dunk yourself seven times in the Jordan River." When Naaman heard those words, he was insulted! *Dunk in the dirty Jordan? Are there not better, cleaner waters?* He was doubly insulted that the Man of God had not come to him personally. But thank God, He always has someone with good sense in the midst! As Naaman turned to depart in his anger, some of his servants said to him, "This is a small thing that the Prophet asks of you, to go, dunk in the water. What have you got to lose?" So Naaman humbled himself and did as he had been instructed by Elisha, and he was healed!

Keep your eyes on Jesus: Hebrews 12:1-3 says, "Let us lay aside every weight and the sin that so easily ensnares us, and let us run with endurance the race that is set before us, looking unto Jesus, the author and finisher of our faith, who for the joy that was set before him endured the cross…" Everything within you might be fighting to do the right thing, while everything that is wrong is pulling at you: *Tell that person off! Lie to your brother! Cheat on your taxes!* But just declare, "I can do all things through Christ who strengthens me!" When you keep your eyes on Jesus, you will never go astray.

Expect God's grace to do what God requires: In 2 Corinthians 12:7-10, Paul speaks of his thorn in the flesh, a problem that troubled him night and day. He went before the Lord three times and asked, "Take this away from me!" But, instead, the Lord gave Paul a revelation. And that revelation is just as valid for you and me today. God said, "My grace is sufficient for you, for My strength is made perfect in your weakness." God's got grace for everything you and I might encounter in life. And that grace, my friend, is all sufficient.

Enjoy the blessings of faith and obedience: James 1:22-25 says, "But prove yourselves doers of the word, and not merely hearers who delude themselves. For if anyone is a hearer of the word and not a doer, he is like a man who looks at his natural face in a mirror; for once he has looked at himself and gone away, he has immediately forgotten what kind of person he was. But one who looks intently at the perfect law, the law of liberty, and abides by it, not having become a forgetful hearer but an effectual doer, this man will be blessed in what he does." The blessing comes not just by hearing the Word but by doing it. And when you do the Word, you will enjoy the blessings that come from the Lord.

These principles will help you live victoriously in whatever situation you face. When difficulties come—and they will—stand on the promises of God. Declare *"I can do this!"*

Think It Through

List two reasons why difficulties arise in our lives: _____
_____
_____

How have you, through Christ, faced a difficulty in your life? _____
_____
_____
_____

List three ways you can overcome any difficulty that comes your way: ___
_____
_____
_____

How does God enable you to carry out the impossible? _____
_____
_____

Why can you boldly declare, "I can do this!" _____
_____
_____

Day 24

Fight Like a Man

"Keep your eyes open for spiritual danger; stand true to the Lord; act like men; be strong; and whatever you do, do it with kindness and love."
~ 1 Corinthians 16:13-14

In 1 Corinthians 16, Paul says to "act like men," but I prefer to say, *"fight like a man!"* At first glance, that may sound gender specific, but that is not the case. When the Corinthians heard Paul speak, they understood exactly what he was saying. He meant "to make brave" or "to be manly" in a spiritual sense; it applies to both genders.

Along with telling the Corinthians to act like a man, be alert, be watchful, stand firm, be strong, and be brave, Paul was also saying, "Let everything you do be done with love." There is no clash between acting like a man and loving. In fact, one of the main definitions of a man is "one who is loving"—who loves his wife, his family, God (first and foremost, of course!), and the ministry. A man is one who loves and loves serving.

In the world, men are taught to be macho, harsh, blunt. The testosterone has to be on display all the time, in a heightened form. But that's not what it means to be a man in the spiritual sense. Anyone can "fight like a man;" they just need to apply these seven biblical steps:

Fight spiritual battles with spiritual weaponry: The mistake we often make is that we try to fight spiritual battles in the flesh, and you can't do it. No matter how much you exercise or bulk up, you are not going to successfully fight a spiritual battle in the flesh. You fight your battles with spiritual weaponry: the weapons of our warfare are not carnal, but mighty through God to pulling down (or demolishing) of strongholds (2 Corinthians 10:4). Fleshly weaponry won't work because people are not our enemies. The Bible tells us that our enemies are principalities, powers, and spiritual hosts of wickedness (Ephesians 6:12). If you're in conflict with anybody, whether it be your spouse, your children, a co-worker--it's really not about that individual. There's a spirit behind the conflict, and so it must be dealt with in the Spirit.

Fight the good fight of the faith: "But you, man of God, run from [ungodliness]. Pursue, instead, righteousness, godliness, faith, love, endurance and gentleness. Fight the good fight of faith, lay hold of eternal life that you were called to and have made a good confession about as well in the presence of many witnesses" (1 Timothy 6:11-12). We're not fighting *for* victory; we're fighting from a position *of* victory. So, we take heaven's victory and enforce it here on earth. The battle has already been won, and Jesus is Lord, amen? I don't care how big and bad the devil may show up looking in life; you don't have to fear him. Fight the good fight of faith, knowing that the outcome has already been determined, even before the foundation of the world. Victory has already been secured; it's been signed in blood.

Fight with focus and determination: "You, therefore, must endure hardship as a good soldier of Jesus Christ. No one engaged in warfare entangles himself with the affairs of this life, that he may please him who enlisted him as a soldier" (2 Timothy 2:3-4). If you have served in the military, you understand that life as military personnel is much different from that of a common civilian. A civilian can choose the time of day that he or she would like to wake up; not so when you're in the military. You have to do whatever they tell you to do. When they say "Get up," you get up. When they say you're going to another country, you go. You belong, in essence, to the military. As a Christian, you are not your own. You have been bought with a price. Whatever He says to do, you must do because He is your Commander-in-Chief.

Fight dressed for success: There are different uniforms for each branch of the military, but when they go out onto the battlefield, they wear clothing that fits the environment—perhaps jungle or dessert fatigues, depending upon what they must face. In Ephesians 6:10-17, Paul wrote, "Be strong in the Lord and in the power of His might, and put on the whole armor of God." He likened our spiritual armor to the attire of a Roman soldier: the helmet of salvation, the breastplate of righteousness, the sword of the Spirit, the shield of faith, the belt of truth, and feet shod with the preparation of the Gospel of peace. You've got to protect yourself, and that is what armor is for!

Fight to the finish: Now I don't know where you are in the fight, but you're not in it to lose it. You did not come this far to give up, my friend, or to end up in defeat. Tell the devil he's a liar. You're not just a survivor, so get out of that survivor mentality into thriving. Stay the course and remember that the Lord has already won the war. And "if God be for us, who can be against us?" (Romans 8:31).

Fight with prayer: There are things that will not change until we pray. The scripture says that men should pray everywhere, lifting up holy hands without wrath and doubting. You should pray every day. Spouses, your loved one needs to see you pray. Parents, your children need to see you pray—and not just at church. Some of my fondest memories are of hearing my mother pray. She'd go into her room, close the door and kneel in prayer. She wasn't trying to be seen or heard. But we would hear her pray. That was influential! And when you pray, God will give you wisdom; when you pray, God will give you strategy. There is power when you pray.

Fight with praise and worship: The same worship that gives praise and glory to God terrifies the enemy. Psalm 144:1 says, "Bless the Lord, my Rock, who trains my hands for war and my fingers for battle." Praise is more than just a physical thing. Every time you raise your hand or wave or clap your hands there's a spiritual dynamic released. If there wasn't, the devil wouldn't try so hard to keep you from doing it. When people are united in praise and worship, it creates a piercing sound that the devil hates. Remember the Israelites at Jericho: after walking around the wall of the city seven times on the seventh day, they shouted and the wall collapsed. When you open your mouth and shout praises to God, walls collapse, too. Things that previously kept you from your blessings collapse. Things that keep you from moving ahead collapse. That's why the enemy doesn't want you to praise. He wants you to fight and bicker with your spouse, your parents, your boss, your co-workers, your neighbors. Don't give in! Praise and magnify the Lord, and you'll be on your way to victory.

Make the determination to "fight like a man" today. When you put these seven principles into action, you will be able to accomplish all that the Lord has for you to do.

Think It Through

According to the Scriptures, our battle is not against flesh and blood, but against what? _____
_____
_____

List some ways you "fight the good fight of the faith": _____
_____
_____

What are some parallels between being a physical soldier and a spiritual soldier? _____
_____
_____

Why is prayer so important to spiritual warfare? _____
_____
_____

List the ways you can "fight like a man": _____
_____
_____

Day 25

Make the Most of Time

"This Book of the Law shall not depart from your mouth, but you shall meditate on it day and night, that you may observe to do according to all that is written in it. For then you will make your way prosperous, and then you will have good success." ~ Joshua 1:8

Today you've been blessed with another day to live. You've got another chance to seize opportunities, to take the plunge, to achieve goals and realize dreams do come true. Aren't you glad to know that? Dreams *do* come true!

You've been given an allotment of time to live here on earth. Unlike God, who is not bound by time, you were created to work within the restrictions of moments, minutes, days, weeks, months and years. As you get older, the days, and even the years, seem to whiz on by! So while you have this time between your earthly sunrise and sunset, I suggest you do as Paul instructed the church at Ephesus (Ephesians 5:15-16): "See then that you walk circumspectly, not as fools but as wise, redeeming the time, because the days are evil." Certainly we can relate to the days being "evil!" Each of us must redeem the time. We must seize every moment and opportunity for Jesus Christ.

Your time must be maximized. The word "maximized" means "made as large as possible, taken advantage of, utilized, made productive, and made fruitful." God wants you to produce. Let's face it: everyone is producing something, but not everything being produced is good for everyone. Some people just produce negative things. You can place some people in a peaceful environment and they will produce conflict.

God wants you to produce a mark on society that is impossible to erase. He wants people to look back over your life and rejoice at the good things you accomplished for Him during your lifetime. Yes, God wants you to produce, but you have to cooperate with Him. This starts with Joshua 1:8. "This Book of the Law shall not depart from your mouth, but you shall meditate on it day and night, that you may observe to do according to all that is written in it. For then you will make your way prosperous, and then you will have good success." You've been enlisted in the process of making your path prosperous and your life of good success. You can't sit idly by. You can't get an attitude with someone else who worked hard, whose life shows the progress you desire. Get your hands dirty; get to work and then you can rejoice in the fruit of your own labor!

No more excuses! Where there's a will, there's a way. I believe God gives you the will, and He will do whatever it takes to fund His mission. No holds barred, no more limits–you need to take the plunge!

There are five important things you must do to maximize your time:

Live on Purpose. Jesus was always clear about His purpose. Remember when He was a child found in the temple? What did He say? "I must be about My Father's business." We're here to be about our Father's business as well. We are to bring glory to the Lord. Myles Munroe said, "Where purpose is not known, abuse is inevitable." I use a microphone on Sundays. I am clear about its purpose: to help amplify my voice so that I can be heard with ease. If I start to bang that microphone like a hammer, I will abuse its purpose. It wasn't designed for that, and most likely I will damage it and eventually destroy it if I continue to use it inappropriately.

Purpose is the original intent of a thing. It is the reason for which something is created or exists. Tom Thiss said, "Having a purpose is the difference between making a living and making a life." According to the Word of God, our purpose is for God's glory, to praise and worship Him with every moment of our lives and to accomplish His will. It's not to work, earn money and pay bills. You need to discover your purpose and walk in it. You must ask, "Lord, what is my purpose?" God will reveal it to you.

Purpose is not what you do for a living, but what you live to do.

Be Prepared. John Wooten contends, "Failing to prepare is preparing to fail." Daily preparation is the key to maximizing lifetime opportunities. Consider the lives of Moses, Joseph and Jesus, who each spent nearly thirty years in preparation for their mission. Educate yourself in your occupation. Enroll in lifetime learning because you know technologies and industries will change. If you're going to keep pace, you need to know what's going on in your world. Whitney Young said, "It is better to be prepared for an opportunity and not have one than to have an opportunity and not be prepared." That's biblical!

Prioritize. Matthew 6:33 instructs us to seek first the Kingdom of God. Seek first His rule and reign, the way He does things. Then everything you need, God will provide. It will be added to you.

You know there's never enough time in a day to do all the things you want to do. It is amazing how busy we are! There will never be enough time to do everything. This is why you need to prioritize and do the most important things first and the least important things last. Stephen Covey said it this way: "Most of us spend too much time on what is urgent and not enough time on what is important." The key is not to prioritize your schedule, but to schedule your priorities.

Learn this word: NO! This one word will help you in your prioritizing. Learn when to say no. If not, people will load you down with things to do.

Be Prudent. Scripture says in Proverbs 14:8, "The wisdom of the prudent is to understand his way, but the folly of fools is deceit." Just a few chapters before, in Proverbs 8:12, we read, "I, wisdom, dwell with prudence and find out knowledge and discretion." Time is one of our greatest assets. You can avoid using time unnecessarily by employing prudence. John Milton noted, "Prudence is that virtue by which we discern what is proper to be done under the various circumstances of time and place."

Don't Procrastinate. Procrastination is the act of willfully delaying the doing of something that should be done. For some people, procrastination is a habitual way of handling any task. These are people who take forever to do the littlest things. Don't put off for tomorrow what you need to do today. Mike Murdock said, "Yesterday is in the tomb, tomorrow is in the womb, and today is all you have." Do what you have to today and make the most of your time.

When it's all said and done, I'm certain you want to hear God say, "Well done, good and faithful servant." What you did in the space of time with your life for His glory and honor will be remembered for eternity. Songwriter Neal Morse, many years ago, penned a powerful song titled "Only What You Do For Christ Will Last." I encourage you to make certain that He is first and foremost in every part of your life and in all you do.

Think It Through

What does it mean to "redeem the time"? _____
_____
_____

Which of the "five ways to maximize your time" are challenging for you? Explain: _____
_____
_____

Do you have trouble saying "No" to people who ask for your help? Why is learning to say "No" so important? _____
_____
_____

Prudence can help you avoid what? _____
_____
_____

Do you procrastinate? If so, how does this affect your use of time?
_____
_____
_____

Day 26

From Glory to Glory

"I will make a road in the wilderness and rivers in the desert."
~ Isaiah 43:19

The natural ear misses spiritual things. It hears only what is audible to it and often overlooks divine announcements. To be successful in this life, it is important that you develop a hearing ear that is in tune with the Spirit of God. You don't want to miss out on what He is doing. It is something far grander than you can imagine!

When you are in tune with the Spirit, you have ears that hear, eyes that see, and a mind that expects that the answers to your prayers will manifest. I believe God is doing a new thing among us, and it would do us well to remember the prophet Isaiah's words in Isaiah 43:18-19, "Do not remember the former things, nor consider the things of old. Behold, I will do a new thing, now it shall spring forth; shall you not know it? I will even make a road in the wilderness and rivers in the desert." God is up to something big-time in your life. Don't miss out on it! See it; embrace it. Do not miss your time of visitation.

The "new thing" God declares speaks to us of a new day and a new way, but it's incumbent upon each of us to respond accordingly and appropriately, to be in sync with the Lord, if this "new thing" is to include us. You and I must do something. We must make changes. Some people are quite rigid, inflexible. Some are so traditionally bound that they think they can contain God in a limited box. I hope you know God can't be contained. He moves in many mysterious ways. Allow God to have His way in your life.

I want God to have His way in my life. I want to experience a new thing, another level of His glory. I want it badly! This is why I keep moving forward. Paul said, "I press on, that I may lay hold of that for which Christ Jesus has also laid hold of me… Forgetting those things which are behind and reaching forward to those things which are ahead…" (Philippians 3:12-14). Don't park here, friend! Keep it moving.

God is doing something in the realm of His Spirit that is leading us into that deeper place. He wants us to experience His revealed glory. In Scripture, the concept of God's glory divides into three main areas: 1) the weightiness of God's manifest presence among His people; 2) God's goodness, wealth and majesty; and 3) the praise, splendor and brilliance of God.

The glory is not about works. In the glory, one finds rest and ease. You cease from your labor and works and simply bask in the presence of God. Psalm 16:11 says, "In Your presence is fullness of joy; at Your right hand are pleasures forevermore." Who wouldn't want to live in His glory?

The ball is in your court. You must synchronize yourself with the purpose of God. There are seven keys to living in His glory. If I were you, I would not treat these lightly. I would give everything I had so that God's glory could be present in my house.

Welcome His presence. I don't go where I'm not welcomed. I don't just show up at people's doors without an invitation. Why would we expect God to show up without an invitation? You need to develop the habit of welcoming Him in. Some people don't welcome Him because they don't really want Him; they just "do God a favor" by worshiping Him in church on Sunday. God doesn't need a favor from anyone! If you want to be stingy in your praise or not even show up to church, that's on you. God has angelic hosts waiting to praise Him. Only those desperate for a move of God will welcome Him into their presence.

Repent. Some Christians are quick to say they don't need to confess sins and repent. I expect their memory is distorted! All unrighteousness is sin. You know the condition of your heart. If your heart's not right with God, you need to repent and change your direction. You need to change your mindset and keep your attention on Jesus Christ.

Humble yourself. Pride will keep you from repenting, and it will keep you from the presence of God. Likewise, God made Himself very clear in 2 Chronicles 7:14, "If My people who are called by My name will humble themselves, and pray and seek My face, and turn from their wicked ways, then I will hear from heaven, and will forgive their sin and heal their land."

You have to pray. Pastor John Kilpatrick was the Senior Pastor of Brownsville Assembly of God in Pensacola, FL, during the time of what came to be known as "The Pensacola Revival." He said that they prayed for two years before revival broke out, expecting that God was doing something. Then they got discouraged. But God moves in the worst of times! It was in this time that God birthed revival at Brownsville. That revival brought millions of souls into the Kingdom and had men, women and children standing in line at 6 a.m. for a 6 p.m. service! If we will get to praying, God will do something explosive in our "worst of times" as well!

Hunger and thirst. Hunger and thirst will motivate you to meet a need. When you seek Him, you will find Him (Jeremiah 29:13). There's no time to play. Give God all of you today. Pursue Him, and when you do,

He'll give you all of Himself. He'll do for you beyond what you can even imagine or fathom!

Walk in the fear of the Lord. To walk in the fear of the Lord is not to walk in terror, but in holy reverence. Practice the presence of God daily. When you're home or on the job, He's right there. It doesn't mean your imperfections will never have opportunity to show up, but if you keep your eyes on Jesus, you will have the power to prevent or minimize negative reactions. Have you ever heard the Lord speak in the midst of a conflict or crisis, directing you not to say a word? This is the work of the Holy Spirit in you to respect His direction. He will fight your battles while you hold your peace.

Minister to the Lord. This is important. Worship is intimacy. The kind of worship the Lord desires is described as "in spirit and truth." God removed the veil so we could enter His throne room, and commune and dine with Him. This is because He wants your worship, not lip service. When you worship actively engaged and with your whole heart, God will transform and inhabit your praises.

2 Corinthians 3:17 says, "Where the Spirit of the Lord is, there is liberty." As you welcome the Lord, humbly repenting and worshiping Him in prayerful passion, the glory cloud will come in. It will be so rich that healings will manifest, situations will be turned around, divorces will be canceled, and the depressed will be freed in their minds! If you hunger after God, I guarantee you: He will do some amazing things in your life.

Think It Through

What is the key to being successful in this life? _____
_____
_____

Which of the seven keys to living in God's glory do you find easy to do?
_____
_____
_____

Which of the seven keys are challenging for you? Explain: _____
_____
_____
_____

How can you overcome the struggles and be released to live "in His glory"? _____
_____
_____

How are "rest" and "ease" associated with God's glory? _____
_____
_____
_____

Day 27
Don't You Dare Give Up!

"Let us not grow weary while doing good, for in due season we shall reap if we do not lose heart."
~Galatians 6:9

Have you ever wanted to throw in the towel and quit? Have you ever thought, "I can't take it any more. I'm done! Stop this world, 'cause I'm gettin' off!" Maybe you tweeted it, #DONE!

If that's ever been the case, or if it's the case today as you read this, I have five words for you: Don't you dare give up! You are too close to your blessing, your breakthrough, your turnaround to walk away now. You're too close to your miracle, too close to give up.

Remember this: Trials come and trials go! Every trial has an expiration date. They will not last forever. An old song says, "I'm so glad trouble doesn't last always." Every one of us has experienced times of testing—those "storms of life" we often hear about. And when they come, you've got to be in balance, get your rhythm and find your flow—and don't park in your trouble. Know that this too shall pass.

You know, not all storms are bad storms. Some storms come to blow your enemies away! When you find yourself in the thick of it, realize that God has a purpose in it. When it's over, you'll be better, wiser and smarter. And while the devil wants you to go through—and look like you've *been* through—God will preserve you.

James said to count it pure joy when we face trials of any kind, because the testing produces perseverance and maturity. If God brought you to it, He's going to bring you through it. Consider it an opportunity to take joy in the God of your salvation, because He is going to bring you out victoriously. You're going to have a testimony that you didn't have before! You've got to see beyond the moment to what lies ahead.

If you're going to remain steadfast through your storm and not give up, there are a few things you must do:

1. **You have to trust the Lord.** This is not optional; it is mandatory. Proverbs 3:5 says, "Trust in the Lord with all of your heart and lean not to your own understanding." Don't lean on your understanding like you would lean on a crutch for support. Verse 6 goes on to say, "In all your ways acknowledge Him, and he will direct your path." In Hebrew, "direct your path" means He'll straighten out what's crooked. We've all got some crookedness in our lives, areas where we're out of alignment. So they need to be straightened. Let God guide and direct you. Acknowledge the Lord in all your ways. This is not only good advice, it's wisdom.

There is nothing that God cannot do. So why worry? Scripture says that with men, some things are impossible; but with God, all things are possible. Trust Him! Jeremiah 32:17 says, "Oh, Sovereign Lord, You have made the heavens and the earth by Your great power and Your outstretched arm. There is nothing too hard for You." Sometimes you just need to remind yourself that God is a way-maker. He'll make ways out of no way. He'll open doors that no man can shut. And He'll shut doors that no man can open.

Find rest in the God of your salvation. You may be in the fiery furnace, but guess what? He's in there with you! You may be in the lion's den, but look around: He's there with you! He will take what was meant for evil and He will turn it around for good.

So, again, I want to encourage you: Don't you dare give up!

2. **You have to be strong**: Your strength will come from having faith and trust in the Lord. This is not an hour to be weak. It is an hour to be strong. But here is the problem: Some of us rely on our own strength. I don't care how much time you spend in a gym or how much protein you take: Your strength can wane. But there is this strength, this supernatural impartation, that comes from the Lord, and that is what you've got to be strong in! If you want to remain, to be steadfast—*if you don't want to give up*—then be who you are! You've been given the power of God. The Spirit of Jesus Christ lives inside you, so "be strong in the Lord and in the power of His might."

3. **You have to pray**: You have to pray *believing*. Some people pray, but they do not believe. They ask, "Oh, Lord, if it be Your will then please do this-or-that." Did you know, you don't need to pray, "If it be Your will" for your loved ones to get saved, because it's the will of God for *all* to be saved? Get in the Word and you'll know to pray according to the Word. You don't need to pray, "If it be Your will, heal my body, Lord," when the Scriptures say, "By His stripes we are healed" (1 Peter 2:24).

If you're praying for a job, you have to pray believing for that job…and you have to cooperate with faith. Don't stay in bed till 2 p.m. and then go look for a job. Get up early! Get your resume together—and dress for success. If the doctors tell you that you're going to have to be on medication for the rest of your life if you don't change your diet, then collaborate with that doctor and cancel that lunch date at your favorite fast food restaurant! You can't eat that kind of food and expect healing to flow to you. Change your diet: eat some vegetables, amen? Cooperate with God.

He's a rewarder of those who diligently seek Him.

These are the things you need to do if you want to stand, if you want to move forward in the Spirit of God: You've got to trust the Lord. You've got to be strong. And then you've got to pray, believing. And one more thing: You've got to praise the Lord anyhow and at all times! Not just in the good times, but in the bad times. I'll admit it: I don't always feel like praising the Lord. But I've learned to train my spirit, my body and my mind to do whatever it takes to praise Him at all times. The only one who doesn't want you to praise the Lord is the enemy, because he knows that whenever you praise, whenever you shout unto God, if you start clapping your hands and dancing in His presence or bowing before Him, you position yourself to be blessed.

Let us magnify the Lord at all times. Remember His goodness, and what He has done for you. And never give up!

Think It Through

Why is it unwise to "park in trouble"? _____
_____
_____

List the three ways that believers can remain steadfast through the storms of life: _____
_____
_____

Do you struggle with any of the above three ways? If so, which ones, and why? _____
_____
_____

Why is it important to back your prayers with actions? _____
_____
_____
_____

What motivates you, as a believer, to "never give up"? _____
_____
_____
_____

Day 28

Don't Fool Yourself

"Don't fool yourself. Don't think that you can be wise merely by being up-to-date with the times. Be God's fool—that's the path to true wisdom. What the world calls smart, God calls stupid. It's written in Scripture, 'He exposes the chicanery of the chic. The Master sees through the smoke screens of the know-it-alls.'" ~1 Corinthians 3:18-20, MSG

Do you know that God wants you to have clarity of purpose? He doesn't want you to be clueless, walking through life aimlessly, not knowing His desires. Quite the opposite! He wants His wisdom and knowledge to be the stability of your life (Isaiah 33:6). He has great plans for you, but those plans require you to obediently follow direction.

It's a shame that so many people think they have the know-how to make quality life choices. We know from Proverbs that a truly wise person will receive wise advice. It's a fool who rejects good counsel (Proverbs 1:5). I caution everyone not to give themselves too much credit. Don't glory in your own intellect. Man's intellect is carnal, and it will ultimately produce negative results. Consider the Lord's words in Jeremiah 29:23-24: "Let not the wise man glory in his wisdom; let not the mighty man glory in his might; nor let the rich man glory in his riches; but let him who glories glory in this, that he understands and knows Me... for in these I delight." Glory in an experiential and intimate knowledge of the Lord.

Not just knowing *about* Him, but truly *knowing* Him.

Hosea 4:6 showcases a terrible problem with God's people: they were destroyed for lack of knowledge. It wasn't that knowledge was unavailable; knowledge was rejected. Similarly, if you reject knowledge today, it will be to your detriment or destruction. The knowledge of the Lord, however, will bless you.

A scripture I take very seriously is found in James 3:13-16. It says, "Who is wise and understanding among you? Let him show by good conduct that his works are done in the meekness of wisdom. But if you have bitter envy and self-seeking in your hearts, do not boast and lie against the truth. This wisdom does not descend from above, but is earthly, sensual, demonic. For where envy and self-seeking exist, confusion and every evil thing are there."

If you insist on doing your own thing, if you promote yourself, if you are envious of someone else's promotion or progress, if you get ahead of God, confusion and every evil thing will be present in your life.

The same passage goes on to say in verse 17 that the wisdom from above is "first pure, then peaceable, gentle, willing to yield, full of mercy and good fruits, without partiality and without hypocrisy." I opt for that heavenly wisdom. I don't want confusion and every evil thing to be present in my life, because I've chosen to reject the wisdom and will of God. I don't want to be like those prophesied to come in 2 Timothy 4:1-5 (AMP). Paul said they would have "itching ears [for something pleasing and gratifying]... to satisfy their own liking and to foster the errors they hold."

Be careful of the company you keep. I like the way Bishop T.D. Jakes puts it: "Whoever has got your ear will affect your head." The wrong voices are cancerous. You, my friend, need to guard your ear gates. Wisdom says that when you're hearing voices, translation and interpretation are vital to avoid miscommunication and misleading. Watch out who you allow to speak into your life. If you're married, don't take the advice of someone who is single and has never been in your position. If you're going through marital problems or a divorce, don't surround yourself with people who are divorced and bitter, still not healed from their own traumas. Remember that Eve was beguiled by a serpent. She let the wrong voice speak into her ear. Then Adam let Eve speak into his ear and they both fell and transgressed against God. Watch who speaks into your ear.

Romans 8:5 tells us, "Those who live according to the flesh set their minds on the things of the flesh, but those who live according to the Spirit, the things of the Spirit." This means you have the choice to be carnally minded (which leads to death) or to be spiritually minded (which leads to life and peace). Don't fool yourself! Those who are in the flesh cannot please God. Now, I don't know about you, but I want everything I do to please Him!

Here are three things you should do to be wise:

1. Keep your mind on Jesus. 1 Peter 1:13 tells us to gird up our minds, being sober and resting our hope fully on the grace we receive with the revelation of Jesus Christ. He is the Author and Finisher of your faith. It is so important to keep Him in "view" at all times!

2. Don't just act spiritual; be genuinely spiritual! Sadly Christians can be some of the greatest actors in the world. Make sure you're not just talking the talk; get in tune with the Spirit and walk the walk! Natural men don't receive the things of the Sprit of God, for they appear to be foolish. But the spiritual person discerns and judges all things, for he or she has the mind of Christ (1 Corinthians 2:13-16). This mind of Christ has been made available to you. It is full of power, wisdom and hope. You simply have to embrace it.

3. Acknowledge the Lord always and in all things. Meditate on Proverbs 3:5-9. The Lord will straighten out the path before you and help you make sense of it all… if you acknowledge Him. You must hear the voice of God and not make a move upon what your flesh senses, sees or feels.

A great way to ensure that you're tuning into the right voices is to first tune into God's voice. Read a chapter of Proverbs every day. There are 31, enough for any month. There's wisdom in this OT book for you, and as you align your perception with the perception of your Heavenly Father, you'll find yourself drawn to those who reflect God's standards.

So my encouragement to you is this: don't insist upon doing your own thing. This is a word you can apply to various areas of your life—your money, your honey, your career, your business. Don't insist on operating by this world's system. It will only bring devastation to you.

Every day you have the same choice to walk in the wisdom of God or the wisdom of this world. You may have missed it before, taking the wrong path and ending up with less than desirable results. Decide today that you will not make a move until you know that you know the Lord has spoken. It will go well for you if you do. Take that necessary time to be certain you're not moving through life on a whim, because, frankly, you don't have the time to waste!

Think It Through

What is "clarity of purpose" and why does God want you to have it?
_____
_____
_____

What are some of the attributes of God's wisdom? _____
_____
_____
_____

List some ways you can keep your mind fixed on Jesus: _____
_____
_____
_____

True spirituality is evident in what kind of behavior? _____
_____
_____
_____

How do you acknowledge the Lord each day? List some ways: _____
_____
_____
_____

Day 29

Power for Living

"It shall come to pass in that day that his burden will be taken away from your shoulder, and his yoke from your neck, and the yoke will be destroyed because of the anointing oil." ~ Isaiah 10:27

Some people mistakenly believe that the Holy Spirit has come just so that they can dance, speak in tongues and have spirited worship services. But Jesus clearly stated that after you receive power—the Greek word, *dunamis*—you will be witnesses. Many Christians don't like to hear that, especially in light of the fact that the word from which we get "witness" means "martyr." It means death. And death is an uncomfortable word to many people, even some Christians. To us, however, it should mean "death to self" or "death to the flesh." But even the flesh dies hard, doesn't it? That's why some believers struggle with relinquishing total control of their lives to Jesus.

In my family, we were taught to say, "Yes, Lord!" We grew up singing it and saying it; because "No, Lord" is a contradiction in terms. He cannot really be Lord if you're telling Him "no." I have discovered that people, even in the church building, will say "yes" to what's good for them. When there's no sacrifice involved, they will say "yes." They'll serve on Sunday, but not on Tuesday night. This walk, however, requires sacrifice. Some people think that "sacrifice" is when we stand on our feet all day, working till our feet get sore. And then we do God a favor by showing up at church for a service or a meeting. When you study biblical sacrifice, you learn quickly that you don't give God something you have left over. You give Him your best! That's the Kingdom way: to give God your absolute best in time, in talent, in treasure. You don't give God what you have left over and think you're doing Him a favor.

God equips us, and He empowers us through the Holy Spirit—but not just for the occasional quickening that leaves us with goosebumps, or even those wonderful times of praising and magnifying the Lord. God gave us the Holy Spirit for much more than having a good time at church.

He gave us the Holy Spirit so that we can have *power for living*…and *power for serving*.

That's why Satan is intimidated when he comes face-to-face with a Spirit-filled, Spirit-led believer. He's not bothered by church-goers. But he is absolutely terrified of those who know the name of Jesus and are filled with the Holy Spirit. He knows the Scriptures better than we do! He knows that Jesus said, "After the Holy Spirit has come upon you, you shall receive *power*," and he knows that "power" is *dunamis*—that dynamite kind of power in believers who recognize the authority they have in Jesus' name. Satan knows they will not be intimidated by him, but will face whatever comes their way and take authority over it. The demons recognize that power, too…and tremble!

The Holy Spirit is not just for Sunday morning, my friend, but for power throughout the week. He wants you to operate in His power in your home, at your job, at school, in the supermarket—wherever you are. When you face the devil or his minions, you want the anointing in your life, because only with the anointing will you be able to drive them out. We often hear "Resist the devil and he will flee." But before that verse it says, "Submit to God." The reason why some believers resist the devil, yet he doesn't flee, is that they aren't submitting to God. When you submit to God—to His will, His desires, His ways—you can tell the devil, "Get out of here!" and he must go, because of that *dunamis* power active in you.

That Holy Spirit anointing which God has given to you is a divine enabling or empowerment; it's of a supernatural nature: it is God's ability on your ability to get the job done. God takes "super" and puts it on your "natural" and makes it "supernatural." He takes "extra" and adds it to your "ordinary" to make it "extraordinary." With this anointing on your life, as Isaiah 10:27 teaches us, burdens are removed and yokes are destroyed. Note that the scripture says yokes are *destroyed*, not broken. Friend, I'm sure you know that if a chair is broken, it often can be repaired and used again. But if the chair is destroyed, throw it out. So the yoke is destroyed; it's irreparable because of the anointing.

To have the anointing truly operating in your life, you must *love righteousness*. God could anoint Jesus with the oil of gladness because He loved righteousness and hated wickedness (Psalm 45:7). Notice that the scripture doesn't say, "hate the wicked." It says, "hate wickedness." You've got to love everybody. Even the people who despitefully use you or the ones who talk about you. You don't have to like what they say or do. But you have to love them…and pray for them. Why? Because Christ loves everybody. That's not easy to do. It can be a real challenge sometimes. But that's our mandate from the Lord: "Love one another as I have loved you" (John 13:34).

You not only need to love righteousness, but you also have to *walk in love*. Just as the Word of God carries the faith of God, the love of God carries the anointing of God. And that anointing is going to cost you something. The anointing oil that God showed Moses wasn't just made from sweet ingredients; there was some myrrh, and myrrh speaks of bitterness.

You say you want to be anointed? How badly do you want it? Because

God is going to usher you into some bitter experiences. People will lie to you, hate you, try to devour you...But you said you wanted to be anointed! If that is true, then you will go through the School of the Holy Spirit, and He will temper you and bring transformation.

In the anointing oil, the component that brings all of the ingredients together is the olive oil. In order to get the oil from the olive, it has to be squeezed. They put stones on it to extract its virtue. It's an uncomfortable place for the olive, but, oh, for the virtue that's released when it's inconvenient, uncomfortable, or when there's squeezing involved, or stretching or stress or anguish.

In the process of the Holy Spirit, you are like the olive oil—you become refined, virtuous, knowing that whatever comes your way, you have power over it, because of the anointing of God! And you walk in love, because how can you say you love God if you hate your fellow man? (1 John 4:20). Love, according to 1 Corinthians 13:4-8, is kind, patient, and long-suffering, among other virtues. Take the time to read that portion of Scripture and let it sink in, because it is so important!

Finally, you need to live a *life of praise and worship*. Don't wait for Sunday service: Get alone with the Lord, tell Him how much you love Him, lift up His Name! The anointing doesn't work in the lives of whiners, complainers, murmurers or ungrateful people. The power of God is not activated in that scenario. It comes when you simply praise and magnify the Lord from a grateful heart.

Seek the anointing of God today. Trust Him to see you through, to fill you and bless you and give you power for living!

Think It Through

What kind of "death" is necessary in order to be a witness for the Lord? Explain: _____
_____
_____

God's "power for living" comes through sacrifice. What does this means to you? _____
_____
_____

Can *dunamis* power be active within you if you're not submitted to God? Explain: _____
_____
_____

How is love tied to the anointing of God in a believer's life? _____
_____
_____
_____

What is the connection between praise and worship and God's anointing?
_____
_____
_____

Day 30

Focus on the Mission

"The harvest truly is great, but the laborers are few; therefore pray the Lord of the harvest to send out laborers into His harvest." ~ Luke 10:2

Every one of us has a calling, a purpose or mission in life. You were created distinctly, and your destiny is equally unique. Only you can do the thing God has commissioned you to do. Not everyone is gifted for business; not everyone is capable of pastoring. If you try to fill a position not designed for you, you will become frustrated with the challenges and lack of progress or satisfaction it brings.

If you are to find the greatest enjoyment in life, you must be in the will of God *for* your life. Discover what your Creator has called you to do or be. You already know from Scripture that it is something far greater than you can imagine, something that will make a mark impossible to erase.

Some are called to government. Some are called to teach. Some find their niche in retail. Some discover their life's purpose with children. Some are given to athletics; some to entertainment. Where are you called? What will you do for the kingdom?

I think of Jesus commissioning the 70 individuals to be apostles in Luke

10:1-12. The applicable principles within these verses show us how to hold to and execute the unique mission God has placed before us.

Recognize the mission. The first step toward holding to your God-given mission is to recognize you have one. You, Beloved, are called, appointed and anointed. Just like the 70, you have been commissioned. The word "commissioned" conveys a proclamation of one's election and induction for a designated purpose.

You didn't have to be perfect to be chosen. 1 Corinthians 1:26-28 reminds us that "Not many wise according to the flesh, not many mighty, not many noble, are called. But God has chosen the foolish... the weak... the base... the despised... that no flesh should glory in His presence." Jesus said, "You did not choose Me, but I chose you and appointed you that you should go and bear fruit, and that your fruit should remain" (John 15:16). He chose you, and your mission is to be productive and useful. Whatever the specific job title or location, embrace your position and produce in it.

Don't go it alone. In Luke 10, Jesus selected the seventy and sent them out two-by-two to be His forerunners. No man is an island. Don't ever be deceived into believing that you don't need anyone else. Divine connections and godly relationships are vital and should be cherished. They provide fellowship, partnership, strength and encouragement.

Some things will only be accomplished by the power of agreement. You may be strong, but you're not strong enough to go it alone. When we walk together, pray together, praise together, serve together, things get done. Jesus said, "Where two or three are gathered in My name... " (Matthew 18:20). Don't allow the enemy to break up the miracle-producing agreement between you and those to whom God has connected you. Isolation is a tool of the enemy to bring disconnection and to sow discord because he knows the power of unity.

Focus! Don't let offenses distract you from your mission. Satan is a scoundrel. He's a deceiver. He will attempt to sway you in a direction opposite the mission God has called you to complete. Focus and never forget the mission. Just like the 70 were to go out before Christ, announcing the ministry of Jesus, your mission isn't about you. It is never about you!

God has given you incredible talent and skill. As I said, your future in God's will is a great one. But it's up to you to turn from pride and keep things in perspective – this mission is not about you; it's about Jesus. Thank Him for the gift, and don't misappropriate it or mistake your goal for one of self-promotion.

Expect great things every day. In regard to your mission, you must expect great doors of opportunity and blessings. You must live in a constant state of expectancy. Jesus said in Luke 10:2, "The harvest is truly great, but the laborers are few." Do you want to be numbered among the few? Then make yourself available to be used and pray that God sends more laborers to work with you.

I believe God is saying there is not only a great harvest of souls ready for ingathering, but there is a great harvest of blessings not *being* prepared, but *already* prepared. God says the stage is set; things are shifting. You must get ready for an explosion in your life. It's reaping time! When you were sowing, you sowed in tears; but now, as you reap, you will reap in joy, bearing the harvest with you (Psalm 126:5).

Don't be afraid. Jesus said in Luke 10:3, "I'm sending you out as lambs among wolves." A lamb is docile with small teeth; a wolf is aggressive and intimidating with sharp teeth. When you see a wolf, remain focused on the mission. God will take care of the wolf. You cannot allow dangerous conditions to frighten you. He has given you a spirit of power, love and a sound mind (2 Timothy 1:7). "No weapon formed against you shall prosper" (Isaiah 54:17). God never said that no weapon would *form*; He said it wouldn't *work!* While it might appear that it's working, there is a reckoning day coming, upon which all things will be done according to God's Word. You can be confident that ALL things work together for good (Romans 8:28).

Don't worry about a thing! "Carry neither money bag, knapsack, nor sandals," Jesus said in verse 4. In other words, you should be so focused on your mission that you're not concerned with things. Your focus must be intentional. As it says in Matthew 6:31-33, don't worry about where you're going to live or work or what you're going to eat. God will take care of you.

Shake off the dust. Jesus said in verses 5-12, "Don't wander; find rest in the place I've sent you. Find peace." I believe many are wasting time with people who do not want to receive what God has sent them to give. My friend, go where you're celebrated and not just tolerated. If you come to a house of rejection, shake the dust off your feet and let it be a witness against that place. Where God is getting ready to take you, you cannot allow the things of past life to cling to you. It might be the dust of a past relationship, a hardship, a lie told against you. Regardless of what it is, you must shake it off. If you don't, it will contaminate your new blessing. Where God is taking you is better than where you've been. Take rejection as a sign. They rejected Jesus; they'll reject you. Just shake it off and keep moving.

Beloved, you are a precious, hand-picked and called individual. Be mindful of your mission, of God and His kingdom, and serve to the best of your abilities. Submit to God saying, "Yes, Lord. Your will be done." If you have struggled with rejection, disappointment, frustration, shame, failure or discouragement, I pray your heart will be encouraged, healed and set free. God is committed to the plans He has for you and *will* perform them unto completion. He will bring things out favorably for you as you stay in His will for your life.

Think It Through

What is your calling, your "unique destiny" in life? _____
_____
_____
_____

Why is it important to live in "a constant state of expectancy" concerning your life's mission? _____
_____
_____

List some things that can distract you from your mission: _____
_____
_____
_____

How can you avoid these distractions? _____
_____
_____

Sometimes, to stay focused on the mission, believers must "shake the dust off" their feet. What does this mean to you? _____
_____
_____
_____

Day 31

Finish Strong

"Fight the good fight of faith, lay hold on eternal life, to which you were also called and have confessed the good confession in the presence of many witnesses." ~ 1 Timothy 6:12

You may have heard the old saying, "The race is not given to the swift or the battle to the strong, but to those who endure to the end." I looked throughout the scriptures for one verse to back this up, but couldn't find it, because it's actually the joining of two verses, Ecclesiastes 9:11 and Matthew 24:13. In principal, this saying is true, and its implications are not only for today, but also for your life—that *you* would finish strong.

I'm sure you know that it's often easier to start something than it is to finish it. Some people start diets, and the first day is wonderful. But after that, they forget to diet and exercise. They say they're going to be a nicer person this year. But they're meaner than they were last year. They say that they're going to get their finances in order. But they're still spendthrifts. They say they're going to be faithful in church and in ministry, in tithes and offerings, and in serving. They start off fine...but they don't finish strong. That's a problem! Don't begin projects with great enthusiasm, then run out of steam right there in the middle.

In Hebrews 12:1 it says, "Therefore we also, since we are surrounded by so great a cloud of witnesses, let us lay aside every weight, and the sin which so easily ensnares *us,* and let us run with endurance the race that is set before us." Here, the writer of Hebrews is telling us that God has a special race for each of us to run; and if you expect to win that race, you've got to start…and then you've got to go on to the finish.

Paul ran his race…and finished strong. He had many opportunities to quit, but he wouldn't. He had obstacles and challenges. All kinds of things happened to him, but he kept on moving. Paul said in 2 Timothy 4:6-8, "For I am already being poured out as a drink offering, and the time of my departure is at hand. I have fought the good fight, I have finished the race, I have kept the faith. Finally, there is laid up for me the crown of righteousness, which the Lord, the righteous Judge, will give to me on that Day, and not to me only but also to all who have loved His appearing."

As I read this passage in 2 Timothy, I realized that if Paul had finished strong, then he certainly could tell us something about how to do it. I've come up with five things we can learn from Paul in order to finish strong:

Fight the Good Fight of Faith: This expression is also found in 1 Timothy 6:12. Here, Paul tells Timothy, his spiritual son: "Fight the good fight of faith, lay hold on eternal life, to which you were also called and have confessed the good confession in the presence of many witnesses." The Greek word translated "fight" is where we get the English word, "agony," and it literally means *to engage in conflict.* The word was used in the context of competing in athletic games; and also for engaging in military conflict. If you've ever been in a military conflict, or some serious athletic competition, you know that you've got to give *all* that you have; you've got to exercise every muscle, even if it means occasionally straining them—so you can finish the race, and finish strong!

Run to Win: 1 Corinthians 9: 24-27 says, "Do you not know that those who run in a race all run, but one receives the prize? Run in such a way that you may obtain it. And everyone who competes for the prize is temperate in all things. Now they do it to obtain a perishable crown, but we for an imperishable crown. Therefore I run thus: not with uncertainty. Thus I fight: not as one who beats in the air. But I discipline my body and bring it into subjection, lest, when I have preached to others, I myself should become disqualified." You need to run like you *want to win*. Run with purpose. Run with vision. I remember something I heard long ago: Winners never quit…and quitters never win. You've got to discipline yourself, if you want to be a winner. You've got to bring your body into submission.

Play by the Rules. In 2 Timothy 2:5, Paul says, "And also if anyone competes in athletics, he is not crowned unless he competes according to the rules." If you want to win this race and complete this journey in life, *you've got to play by the rules*. Rules and boundaries, not just skills and talents, are what make the game interesting. Think about it: If there were no rules or boundaries, if you just did whatever you wanted to do, you really wouldn't have a game. You'd just be playing. If you're going to run this race and win, then you're going to have to do it God's way. You're going to have to be just like Jesus, even in your own Gethsemane experience. When it gets down to the place of pressing, "nevertheless, not my will, but Your will be done." Play by the rules!

Run with Endurance. In Hebrews 12:1-2 we read, "…let us run with endurance the race that is set before us, looking unto Jesus, the author and finisher of our faith, who for the joy that was set before Him endured the cross, despising the shame, and has sat down at the right hand of the throne of God." Lay aside every weight and every sin. Remember, God didn't come to bring condemnation, but salvation to the world. God loves us so much He doesn't want us to stay in a messy place. He doesn't want us to be unfinished. He's begun something good in us; but God will test us, so that we can be developed and mature. That's why God puts some people in our lives that, quite frankly, we'd rather do without! He wants to teach us things we need to know, in order to run that race with patience and endurance. Run with Jesus! Don't run *from* Him; run *with* Him! Jesus knows the track. As Paul said, run with your eyes fixed on Him! Not only should you look *at* Him while your run *with* Him, but look *to* Him, as an example, "who for the joy that was set before Him endured suffering and shame on the cross."

Press on. In Philippians 3:12, Paul says, "Not that I have already attained..." Now, some people think they've already arrived. They may not say it, but they act like it. The truth is, none of us have arrived. We all have a ways to go, my friend. There's still something more we have to learn about Him; there's still something more we need to learn about us. There's still more we must do. And more we must say. We have *not* arrived! If you think you have arrived, then you will quit. We can't park here thinking that this is it: we've got another place to go, another level and another dimension to go. But if we think we've already made it, then we'll miss it, and we'll never be motivated to press on. Remember what Paul said: "Forgetting those things that lay behind me, I must press toward the goal" to obtain the prize. So take note: we must press past our past. Everybody's got a past. No matter how far back your past, or how recent, you've got to forget; you've got to let it go or it's going to hold you back. You've got to press on past your past and toward your future—and the goal of the prize. The past that Paul refers to is not just the negative things; it's the positive things, as well. If you get stuck on what you did years ago, even the good things, and park there, you'll never get anywhere today.

Move past the positives. Thank God for them, but you've got to keep on moving ahead. Forget what's behind you... Forgetting is not amnesia, denial or avoidance! Forgetting, in this context, is putting the past in proper perspective and moving on, despite the pain or the pleasure. Invite the Lord to make your past count for your future. Know that everything in your life—the good, the bad and the ugly—God can and will use it to make your past a present for your future.

Think It Through

Explain how the "fight of faith" is similar to a military conflict or athletic competition: _____
_____
_____

Many people struggle with self-discipline. Explain why it is so important to "winning the race" of faith: _____
_____
_____
_____

Why are God's rules and boundaries so important to winning the race?
_____
_____
_____

How do you "run with endurance"? _____
_____
_____
_____

Have you "pressed past your past," or are there things which are slowing you down? Explain: _____
_____
_____
_____

GODZCHILD PUBLICATIONS

Made in the USA
Middletown, DE
24 November 2019